English for Academic Research

Series Editor
Adrian Wallwork, English for Academics
Pisa, Italy

This series aims to help non-native, English-speaking researchers communicate in English. The books in this series are designed like manuals or user guides to help readers find relevant information quickly, and assimilate it rapidly and effectively. The author has divided each book into short subsections of short paragraphs with many bullet points.

Adrian Wallwork

AI-Assisted Writing and Presenting in English

Springer

Adrian Wallwork
English for Academics
Pisa, Italy

ISSN 2625-3445 ISSN 2625-3453 (electronic)
English for Academic Research
ISBN 978-3-031-48146-8 ISBN 978-3-031-48147-5 (eBook)
https://doi.org/10.1007/978-3-031-48147-5

This Springer imprint is published by the registered company Springer Nature Switzerland AG
The registered company address is: Gewerbestrasse 11, 6330 Cham, Switzerland

Paper in this product is recyclable.

Introduction

Why this book? How can AI writing tools benefit me?

This volume focuses on how to use AI, specifically large language models (LLMs), to write in English. The book covers how to use LLMs with research papers, emails to fellow academics, cover letters, rebuttal letters, texts for lay audiences, and scripts for presentations. It shows you when you can and cannot trust LLMs to carry out specific tasks. The book does NOT recommend using LLMs to write an entire paper (see 9.10).

A key issue with LLMs is that currently they have no menu, and this is why users may not be able to understand their full potential. This thus requires users to be creative and to instinctively know what prompts to ask a chabot-this book will teach you how.

> Note: Tools such as ChatGPT are technically called *large language models*. However, for the purposes of this book I use the terms *LLMs*, *bot* and *chatbot* to mean the same thing.

THE PROS OF LARGE LANGUAGE MODELS

As a researcher, you can save yourself a lot of effort if you use a chatbot to help you write in English. This books suggests two ways of doing this:

1. Write in your language, edit what you have written to make it English-ready, submit it to machine translation, and check the output.
2. Write directly in English using a chatbot to suggest content, and also to correct what you have written. This involves learning what prompts to use.

My tests with PhD students have shown that these two methods generally produce a more accurate text than writing directly in English without the aid of LLMs.

So the English will be accurate. But this does not necessarily mean that your text i) matches the criteria for good readability; ii) satisfies readers expectations from a content point of view; or iii) is written well, i.e. of a good quality.

THE CONS OF LARGE LANGUAGE MODELS

Large language models **cannot** do everything. For instance, if you are writing a research paper, there are currently **NO** tools that can 100% differentiate between essential and non-essential corrections to your English, tell you that you need to highlight your key findings more clearly, or that you have often used synonyms for key words. Without a lot of prompting, a chatbot cannot tell you that what you have written is tedious and full of vague terms and concepts, that you have plagiarized yourself or others, that you have written far too much, that you have failed to mention any limitations in your research, and that the reviewers are likely to criticize your work. Other types of tools, such as Grammarly and Writefull, while generally doing a good job at correcting English, are currently unable to do much of the work that a human editor can do. They also have some basic issue with the use of tenses, countable and uncountable nouns, spotting ambiguity, distinguishing between key and non-key words, dividing up long sentences and paragraphs.

Consequently the book also tells you when a better option would be to contact a professional translation / editing service.

This book is part of the *English for Research* series of guides for academics of all disciplines who work in an international field. To be able to benefit fully from this book, it helps if you have an upper intermediate level (B2) of English. Within the book there are many links to the other books in the series to enable you to study particular topics more in depth.

Which tools/models are analyzed?

Most of the examples in this book were generated by ChatGPT and Google Translate. But the guidelines and examples given apply to other chatbots and machine translation tools. People have their personal preferences as to which tools do the best job. When giving prompts, I strongly suggest that you consistently use a mix of chatbots, as they often provide different answers in different formats. You have a wide choice that includes Gemini, Copilot, Poe, Claude, and Perplexity. Tools such as Grammarly, Reverso, and QuillBot, can be effective but have a much more limited use, and are thus only touched on in passing in this book. At the time of writing this book, Grok and AJE's tool Curie were not available, but the latter is definitely worth checking out if you need to edit an entire paper.

Practically everything I say about Google Translate is also true of DeepL, which I have found to be an excellent machine translator.

What are the advantages of the pro models?

At the current state of the art, for the purposes of improving and correcting your English, I personally think the free versions are sufficient.

Structure of the book

Chapters 1–9 of this book are primarily intended for **non-native researchers**, but will also be useful for native speakers. Chapter 1 is a key chapter as it outlines exactly what a bot can and cannot do at the time of writing this book (summer 2023). Obviously, AI is still very much in its early days, and AI may soon be able to carry out some of the tasks that I mention as not being currently possible.

Chapter 9 is also for **professional language editors/translators**, who can indirectly learn how their professional work adds value for their clients.

Chapters 10 is for **EAP teachers**, who will learn how to

- use AI to its full potential as a translator and editor
- differentiate their service as an editor or translator from an AI tool
- use chatbots and automatic translation in a course for teaching academic English to non-natives

The main skills to learn for both native and non-natives are how to

- write a good prompt
- pre-edit a text for translation
- check/correct/improve the output of a chatbot or a machine translation

The book does not cover any ethical issues associated with AI, nor does it cover AI applications and general software that are not directly related to writing skills.

Contents

Chapter 1
Being realistic about what AI can and cannot do

1.1 Introduction

Large language models (LLMs), which with reference to models such as ChatGPT I also refer to as *chatbots* or *bots*, often seem to be smarter than they are: they can generate essays and emails, they can simulate a job interview, they can give accurate answers to most questions.

In fact, users often tend to interact with chatbots as if they were humans, even referring to the bot as *him* or *her*. The danger is that you will get frustrated when things go wrong and attribute the blame exclusively to the chatbot, rather than to the fact that the prompt you used may not have been ideal. In any case, like humans, they do make mistakes.

Moreover, they cannot do some of the basic things that a human can do, e.g. distinguish between an 'essential' and 'non-essential' correction in terms of English language use, or avoid changing key words even when asked several times not to do so. Apparently very specific prompts to reduce a text "by exactly 50 words" are beyond its powers: it will reduce the text instead by a totally random number of words or reduce it to a total of 50 words. So a chatbot may seem intelligent if you ask it to define an 'essential' correction or a 'key word' - it comes up with very articulate bulleted definitions. But in reality it relies on finding matching patterns in its database and in repeating knowledge in much the same way as a parrot.

However, this book would not have been written if I didn't think that LLMs could seriously help you to improve the accuracy of your English.

A. Wallwork, *AI-Assisted Writing and Presenting in English*, English for Academic Research, https://doi.org/10.1007/978-3-031-48147-5_1

This book primarily focuses on the various ways a bot **CAN** help you in all areas of writing in English – Chapters 2–8. Within those chapters, it also mentions those areas where a bot fails to do or simply **CANNOT** do what you would like it to do.

Section 1.2 of this chapter summarizes what a chatbot is able to do without too much difficulty. Then the focus moves to areas of good writing that **LLMs are currently unable to help** you with. Essentially, automatic translation and chatbots are excellent at producing accurate English. But if the text they are working on is not well written in terms of style, structure, and content (rather than in terms of the use of English), LLMs cannot miraculously transform it. So this chapter focuses on those areas that you need to work on yourself, rather than relying on artificial intelligence.

1.2 What a chatbot CAN generally do reliably

Chatbots can considerably improve your writing skills and also help with preparing presentations.

If prompted correctly (Chapter 2), ChatGPT can generally be depended on to carry out all of the following fundamental tasks, while applications such as Grammarly and Writefull are limited above all to points 1–7.

1. Correct grammar mistakes.
2. Identify where punctuation needs adding.
3. Paraphrase and summarize.
4. Make suggestions on improving the content and style of your text.
5. Make phrases more concise.
6. Transform passive to active sentences.
7. Make recommendations for the title of your paper.
8. Transform a structured abstract into an unstructured one and vice versa.
9. Help write all the various sections of a paper.
10. Generate a script for a presentation.
11. Generate suggestions for what to put on slides on the basis of your script.
12. Generate emails.
13. Make suggestions/comments regarding emails that you have written.
14. Make suggestions on how to appeal to a lay audience.
15. Role play specific academic scenarios (e.g. socializing at a conference, going to a job interview).

1.3 What a chatbot MAY or MAY NOT do

Bots are not consistent. You can give them a prompt one day and the bot will do as requested. The next day with the same prompt, it may be less obedient! You need to be aware that it is often difficult to:

1. Control the type and number of modifications that a bot will make.
2. Stop the bot from making possibly illogical connections between sentences by introducing link words such as *meanwhile*, *in contrast*.
3. Stick to the same prompt, even when you instruct it to do so.
4. Stop it from generating very generic statements, particularly when prompted to write emails without specifying the maximum number of words.
5. Get it to reduce the length by a <u>specific</u> number of words.
6. Prompt it to consistently break up long paragraphs into shorter ones.
7. Get it to vary the length of sentences. Bots tend to only produce sentences of 20–30 words.
8. Discourage it from always starting a text with an introduction and ending it with a conclusion that basically repeats the introductory sentence.

1.4 What a chatbot CANNOT do in terms of writing research papers

There are some areas of writing and editing a paper that only a human professional can be relied upon to do. These areas include the following vital points where chatbots regularly fail to be of assistance.

1. Provide a <u>complete</u> list of all the changes it has made to your text and why it has made such changes, even if specifically prompted to do so.
2. Differentiate between 'essential' and 'non-essential' – a bot has no idea what an essential correction consists of, even if you try to train it.
3. Highlight your key findings for you in a way that will make them stand out for the reader.

4. Clarify cases where you have not been explicit with regard to what you have found and others have found.
5. Highlight cases where you have used a synonym for a key word.
6. Advise you when you have written too much.
7. Identify a potentially ambiguous phrase.
8. Automatically warn you when you have used biased or inappropriate language, or non-gender-neutral pronouns.
9. Warn you that you have plagiarized yourself or others.
10. Anticipate possible opposition by your referees and readers by suggesting that you 'hedge' a very strong affirmation or you discuss the limitations of your research.

1.5 What are the main pros and cons of machine translation?

If you speak a major European language, machine translation (MT) of academic texts into English is generally as good as a human translator – there are really no cons. However, MT can only achieve the levels of a human translator if you work on the original text in your own language. This work is called pre-editing (Chapter 3). If you speak Chinese, Turkish, Arabic, Hindi, i.e. major languages but not European, then MT is not as accurate and may produce sentences in English that appear to have no sense. However, if you pre-edit your text in the ways suggested in Chapter 3, then MT will enable you to produce a good first draft, and the time you save by using MT you can spend on thorough post-editing (Chapter 4).

MT only translates, it cannot help you with any of the points mentioned in 1.4.

1.6 The difficulties non-native speakers have within academia

An article published in The Conversation (theconversation.com) and entitled *Non-native English speaking scientists work much harder just to keep up* reported some of the results from a survey by the translatE project. Compared to native English-speaking researchers, the survey (which predated ChatGPT) found that non-native researchers

1. take 91% more time to read a paper in the literature
2. need 51% more time to write a paper
3. have their papers rejected 2.6 times more frequently, and are asked for revisions 12.5 times more frequently
4. take 94% longer to prepare for a presentation at an international conference
5. are 50% less likely to decide to give an oral presentation, and 30% less likely to attend a conference

The article highlighted that the costs involved for a non-native academic to have their paper professionally edited or to attend a conference are often too much for them to bear – so they miss out, and as a consequence the scientific community misses out on the research that these academics are doing. In fact, the results of the translatE project demonstrate that much of the information that is published in non-English journals would be fundamental to 'solving global challenges such as the biodiversity crisis'.

Today, however, AI can completely or partially resolve the five issues listed above.

READING

The length of time to read someone's else's paper (91% more for non-natives according to the survey), can now easily be resolved by AI. If you have a paper to read in English, and your native language is say, Spanish, then just get Google Translate (DeepL etc.) to translate it for you. It takes a couple of minutes. Of course this implies two things: (i) the article is in a digital format; (ii) Google covers your language and is not one that is only spoken by a minority of people (i.e. with an insufficient database for Google to draw from).

WRITING

Second statistic: 51% longer to write. There are two ways in which AI can solve this problem. First, you could write in your own language, pre-edit it as suggested in Chapter 3, and translate it automatically into English. This seems to me to be a very simple option, and because of the pre-editing stage you would probably end up taking 10% more time to write than a native speaker. Of course you would need to check that the automatic translator had not made mistakes (just as you would have to check for mistakes if you had written it directly in English).

Alternatively, you could write it in English and then submit it to ChatGPT for correction – see Chapters 2 and 4. This second option will certainly take longer to produce a final paper than if a native speaker was writing it, but less than 51% longer.

REJECTIONS AND REVISIONS

The article in The Conversation doesn't specify whether or not the rejections and requests for revisions were based exclusively on language factors or not. In any case it is undoubtedly true that non-natives have their papers rejected more frequently, and there is a lot of literature that supports it.

In my 30 years as a scientific editor I have seen many papers that have been rejected due to 'poor English'. Poor English covers a massive terrain including: typos, grammar errors, syntax etc, and in such cases the reviewer is likely to give some examples to prove their case. But 'poor English' is often used as a polite way of saying: "you haven't really said very much, and what you have said doesn't really make a huge amount of sense". I would contend that a paper that gets rejected for poor English might have been rejected even if the author had written it in their native language and had submitted it to a journal with the same readability and scientific requirements as the English journal that rejected it. I am not saying that this is always the case, but it does happen. It also happens to native speakers, but in this case the comment is likely to be 'poor structure' or 'general lack of coherence'.

AI alone is not a sufficient aid to ensure that your paper will be accepted and will overcome the rigidity of some referees, but it can certainly help.

PRESENTATIONS AND CONFERENCES

A key reason why many non-natives do not attend conferences is cost AI can do little about this, but the scientific community can, by subsidizing such researchers.

However, AI can help with the preparation of presentations, it can help you produce a perfect script in English, it can help you learn how to pronounce every word in your script, it can suggest a structure, it can generate content for your slides (text, tables, figures, images). Native speakers are also already using many of these features. To learn how to do this, see Chapter 6.

1.7 Using chatbots to identify what editors are looking for

Below are some of the typical things that editors are looking for in manuscripts to enable them to keep their readership levels high.

TYPE OF PAPER	Original research, or a systematic review, or a position paper etc (for more on the various types of papers consult Google Scholar or Wikipedia).
SUBJECT	Hot topic (contemporary issues), original and innovative.
AIM	Clarity of purpose, i.e. the research objectives are clear.
RESEARCH	Well conducted, methodology clear, ethical, reproducible, no bias, limitations highlighted.
RESULTS	In line with research objective; entirely new or confirmation of other results already published in the same journal; not too broad; can be generalized outside your very specific field.

The most obvious way to find out what kind of paper your journal wishes to receive, and the kind of style and format it should be written in, is to go directly to the site of the specific journal. Below is the link to such information for Nature.

https://www.nature.com/nature/for-authors/editorial-criteria-and-processes

However, you can also get ideas by consulting ChatGPT. Below is what ChatGPT generated with regard to what Nature is looking for. The **prompt** was:

> **I want to write a paper for Nature. What kind of papers will be the editor be looking for?**

I am reporting it here (i) to show you an example of how ChatGPT can help you as an academic, (ii) because what the bot writes is true of the requirements of most journals, so you can learn from it:

Originality and Innovation: Nature seeks papers that present novel and groundbreaking findings. Your research should push the boundaries of current knowledge, introduce new concepts, or challenge existing paradigms. The paper should clearly articulate the novelty of the work and how it advances the field.

Significance and Impact: The research presented in the paper should have a significant impact on its field or even beyond. It should address important questions, solve critical problems, or lead to new insights with broader implications.

Broad Appeal: Nature aims to publish papers that are of interest to a wide range of researchers across various disciplines. Your paper should be written in a way that makes it accessible to scientists from different backgrounds, not just specialists in your field.

Clear and Engaging Presentation: Your paper should be well-organized, with a clear and concise structure. Make sure your writing is engaging and easy to follow. Visual aids such as figures, graphs, and diagrams can help convey your findings effectively.

Robust and Rigorous Methodology: The methods you used to conduct your research should be robust and rigorous. Your experiments or analyses should be designed and executed meticulously to ensure the reliability and reproducibility of your results.

Data and Evidence: Your paper should present substantial and compelling evidence to support your conclusions. This evidence could include experimental data, statistical analyses, simulations, or any other relevant forms of empirical support.

Interdisciplinary Connections: Nature appreciates research that bridges different scientific disciplines. If your work has the potential to connect ideas from multiple fields, it might be especially appealing.

Clarity of Impact Statement: In your paper, make sure to clearly state the broader impact and significance of your findings. How will your research change the way scientists think or impact real-world applications?

Conciseness: Nature papers typically have strict word limits, so you need to convey your research and its importance succinctly. Every word should contribute to the paper's overall impact.

Previous Literature: Your paper should provide context by discussing relevant existing literature. Explain how your work builds upon or contrasts with previous research in the field.

The bot will produce a similar list of points for whatever journal name you submit. Even if ChatGPT is 'not aware of' chosen journal, it can still give you general insights on what editors might look for in papers submitted to a journal in your discipline. It also warns you to consult the journal's official guidelines.

1.8 AI cannot tell you how to highlight your key findings

One of my students once received the following comment by a referee as a justification for rejecting her paper: *Not acceptable. No new knowledge, science or discovery is presented.* This kind of comment may reach you even six months after you have sent your paper for review. For you, it represents a considerable waste of time and energy spent on a paper.

Before you start writing, be clear in your head about:

- The overall aim of your research.
- The most significant findings you've obtained and how you can establish their validity.
- How these discoveries deviate from, and contribute to, existing knowledge.

The significance of your findings may be evident to you due to months or even years of dedicated work. But the reader is coming to these findings for the first time – give the reader a clear message.

While deciding the content for each section of your paper, think about exactly where and how you could emphasize your unique contribution. Where: in what sections of your paper, and where within these sections. How: through clear unambiguous writing, within a short sentence and within a short paragraph etc.

The reader is going to be asking themself very similar questions to the points I mentioned above:

- What is the specific issue that this paper is trying to address or explore?
- How did the authors approach and tackle this problem?
- In what way does their approach stand apart from previous methodologies?
- What revelations did their investigation yield?
- How do their findings diverge from the existing literature, and what implications do they carry?

Preemptively addressing these questions within your paper will help to ensure that your key findings are clearly highlighted and the significance of your contribution is effectively communicated.

It is difficult to find a way for AI to do this job for you. In any case, it is a process that you need to go through in preparation for the times when you have to present your research orally.

1.9 AI cannot tell you that your style of writing breaks all the rules of readability

Below is an author's attempt at describing how their paper is organized into sections. To retain anonymity, I have replaced the key words with XYZ, A and B.

> *The manuscript unfurls in the following manner: the succeeding section delves into the theoretical scaffolding employed for the analysis, pinpointing the context of the XYZ as significant for evaluating alignment and misalignment among A and B. The third segment delineates the espoused methodology, elucidating both the mechanisms of data gathering and processing. The penultimate part reveals the discoveries and postulates the theoretical and managerial connotations of our results. The concluding remarks encapsulate the primary revelations of the study, sketching its constraints and identifying the necessity for continued exploration.*

The problems with the above description of the structure of the paper are:

1. the choice of words often sounds pompous or is unnecessarily academic (*espoused, theoretical scaffolding, delineate, postulate, connotations, encapsulate*)
2. some words are not appropriate or are ungrammatical (*unfurls, succeeding, among*)
3. synonyms are used for no reason – a paper is always divided into what is commonly known as 'sections', so there is no need to use different words (*segment, penultimate part, concluding remarks*)
4. it would be much easier for the reader if the author wrote *Section 1 … Section 2 …* etc
5. it is very long (90 words)

A bot can only resolve three of the problems listed above. The improvements in terms of problems 1 and 2 are highlighted in normal script in the bot's response below.

The manuscript unfolds in the following manner: The subsequent section delves into the theoretical framework used for the analysis, emphasizing the significance of the XYZ context in assessing alignment and misalignment between A and B. The third segment outlines the employed methodology, elucidating the data gathering and processing mechanisms. The penultimate section presents the findings and discusses the theoretical and managerial implications of our results. The concluding remarks summarize the key revelations of the study, outline its limitations, and underscore the need for further exploration.

The bot has replaced all the words that are of uncommon use. However, the unnecessary synonyms are still there (point 3), there are no section numbers (4), and it is only three words shorter (5).

My first **PROMPT** to the bot was:

Correct and improve this academic text.

To then solve problem 5, i.e. to reduce the length, I followed up with this prompt:

Please reduce the length by 20 words.

The bot then returned this:

The manuscript follows this structure: The next section explores the theoretical framework, emphasizing XYZ's role in assessing alignment between public entities and private corporations. The third part outlines the methodology, detailing data gathering and processing. The penultimate section presents findings and their implications. The conclusion summarizes key findings, limitations, and the need for further exploration.

Much shorter, better and clearer, but problems 3 and 4 remain. You may say that using *part* instead of *section* is not going to confuse anyone. This may be clear, but it will definitely be 100% clear if each sentence begins: *Section 1* ... *Section 2* etc.

Here is the version edited by a human. The human editor has cut the original text by one third with no loss of meaning.

The manuscript is structured as follows. Section 2 examines the theory behind the analysis, highlighting the context of the XYZ. Section 3 outlines the methodology, including the data collection and processing. Section 4 reveals the findings and looks at the theoretical and managerial implications of our results. Section 5 concludes the paper and identifies the limitations and possible future research.

The point is that a bot can only help you to do what it knows how to do: correct, paraphrase, summarize, reduce. The bot cannot tell you that:

- writing an academic paper is not an opportunity for showcasing your writing skills
- your style is inappropriate and your use of vocabulary is bizarre
- you could be a lot clearer in your layout
- you have written far too much

1.10 AI is not enough: You need good writing skills, which you can learn by studying other well-written articles

The bot can help you with the overall structure of a paper, it can even generate an example for you, or it can correct a text that you have submitted.

But AI tools can only do a certain amount to improve your English and your papers – see Chapters 3 and 4.

If the version of your text in your original language (or the text you have in your head when writing directly in English) is poorly expressed or structured then this will mean that editors, reviewers and readers are likely to have difficulty i) reading it, and ii) assessing its value.

One way you can learn good writing skills is looking at articles written by good writers.

Some of the best are written in the MIT Technology Review, an independent journal published by the Massachusetts Institute of Technology. This Review is not a scientific journal where researchers publish their papers. Instead it is a collection of thought-provoking articles on recent advances in the scientific world, written by people who really know how to write and keep their readers with them.

By reading the Review you will learn a host of useful skills that will improve those the parts of your writing that AI has the most difficulty with: sentence/paragraph/article structure and readability (including enjoyability).

You may object that the Review is not sufficiently technical and does not have to describe the technical stuff that you have to, and that your papers require a different type of writing and are for experts in the field.

I would contend that there are certain elements of good writing that are applicable to any text. The reader should be able to follow the logical buildup of arguments without having their brain unduly taxed along the way.

Also, bear in mind that the Review could have adopted a style that was really complex, and their readers would still have had the intellectual capacity to understand it. Instead, they opted for simplicity.

Their mission is: *to make technology a greater force for good by bringing about better-informed, more conscious technology decisions through authoritative, influential and trustworthy journalism.*

The result is that they talk about interesting technical advances in a way that is as accessible and enjoyable as possible, leaving readers feeling they want to know more.

The next subsection outlines some elements of the style of a typical article in the MIT Technology Review.

1.11 AI is not enough: Good style is difficult to achieve with a bot

Below are six key skills of writing that you can pick up by reading high quality journals such as the MIT Technology Review. No chatbots can currently generate a text in such a clear way.

1. Short sentences: generally under 20 words, rarely more than 30.
2. Short paragraphs: around 60 words
3. Because sentences and paragraphs are short, there is less need for punctuation. There are very few semicolons. Instead the writers occasionally use punctuation marks that attract the readers' eyes – hyphens for example are great as they have more space directly above and below and are physically longer than other punctuation marks (they are the length of three or four commas or periods). The reader's eye is attracted by sudden white space in the middle of a sentence, so they will be more inclined to read what is written there.
4. No phrases such as *It is worth noting that*, because it is assumed that everything in the text is worth noting. Also, when something is indeed particularly interesting or a new concept is being addressed, the reader's attention is attracted through tricks such as beginning a new paragraph, or writing an unusually short sentence.
5. The words chosen do not distract you. This means that non-key words are chosen to be as short as possible, e.g. *but* and *yet* rather than *nevertheless* and *however.* There are no unnecessary adverbs or adjectives, no series of nouns all meaning the same thing.
6. Some link words and phrases such as *on the one hand … on the other hand, in addition, moreover* etc do not feature. This is because the purpose they purportedly serve – connecting ideas – is achieved simply by writing in a logical way, where it is clear how and why one sentence or paragraph is connected to the next.

The Review has a strict word count on the length of an article. It has to fit exactly to a page. Given that most people, even great writers, tend to write too much, the word count means that they have to review their draft text, cutting out any excess words or information. Yet when the reader reads the text there is no sense that anything is missing or that anything has been cut. And it is likely that the final text reads better than the longer draft text.

Some elements of the style used by the Review's writers may go against the conventions that you have learned in your own language. For instance, in the Review *and* and *but* are frequently used not just at the beginning of sentences (shock horror), but also at the beginning of paragraphs. Yet some journal editors are still debating as to whether a comma can ever be preceded by a comma or not, i.e. they are focusing on form (with rules being dictated by 'experts' and academies of centuries ago) rather than thinking, might this punctuation device actually help the reader absorb information more quickly?

Just as today's scientists are encouraged to think outside the box when conducting their research, the same out-of-the-box thinking needs to be used to question a hyper-conservative writing style that pays tribute to the past but does not match the way we read today.

I believe that if you really want a successful career in academia and you are really motivated to share your results to make the world better, then you need to write in a way that is not only informative for the reader, but also enjoyable.

You can learn more about the strategies need to write a good paper in the companions to this book

English for Writing Research Papers

English for Research: Usage Style, and Grammar

1.12 What are risks involved in using a bot to correct a research paper?

For decades non-native English speaking researchers have been sending their papers, without any professional editing by native experts, for possible submission in international journals. Some are accepted, many are not. Manuscripts are not necessarily rejected for reasons connected with the use of the English language, but also for the reasons outlined in 1.4 and 1.8–1.10.

So it has always been a risk to submit a paper without having it edited by a professional.

AI reduces the risk of a paper being rejected for 'poor English grammar'. ChatGPT can make a lot of useful corrections listed in 1.2, which makes it an effective tool to correct / improve your English.

If you speak a major European language, then you are likely to incur fewer risks in terms of the accuracy of the English when submitting for publication a machine translated text (but ONLY IF use the tips given in Chapter 3) than you would if you submitted a text written by you directly in English, but which has not been edited by a professional native speaker.

There is of course a risk that AI – chatbots and machine translators - will actually introduce some errors, but I would say that a chatbot will certainly remove more errors than it will introduce. It is also probably easier for you to spot the errors introduced by AI, than it is for you to spot the errors you yourself made in English.

So if you cannot afford the services of a professional editing agency (see Chapter 9 for the benefits of using such a service) overall it is worth using AI as an aid. You will reduce the risk of a journal reviewer rejecting your paper for poor use of English grammar.

Although AI can certainly improve your use of grammar and vocabulary, for the moment it **CANNOT** replace a human editor in terms of improving the quality of the writing. By 'writing' I don't mean the grammar or vocabulary, but the style and readability (1.8–1.11). You can certainly improve your style and level of readability by yourself, but this is something that you have to work on diligently (see Chapters 2–8 in the companion volume: *English for Writing Research Papers*, 2023 edn.). You have to be critical of your own work, and currently without a lot of very specific prompts from a bot (2.7), it is difficult for AI to do this critical assessment for you.

Note: My advice is absolutely **NOT to write an entire paper** using a chatbot. Just use a chatbot to check the English of a paper you have already written. You can also try using AJE's Curie, which was not available at the time of writing this book and is therefore not discussed here. See 9.10 on why you need to be **transparent** about your use of AI.

Chapter 2
Prompts for correcting or paraphrasing your English

2.1 Introduction

There is no single correct way to write a prompt. The same prompt will produce different responses with different bots or even with the same bot. At the time of writing, there is no magical formula.

The chapter begins with a glossary of words that are often associated with the craft of writing prompts – skip this if you are already very familiar with prompting. It then continues by detailing how to write an effective prompt in two main cases, when you want the bot to correct/improve or paraphrase a text that you have already written in English.

2.2 What is a prompt? A glossary

A prompt is an instruction or description designed to get a bot to perform a certain task for you.

The process of writing/structuring a prompt that can be interpreted and understood by an AI model, and then adjusting it on the basis of the bot's output, is known as 'prompt engineering'. Various terms are used in prompt engineering which have been borrowed from other disciplines:

A. Wallwork, *AI-Assisted Writing and Presenting in English*, English for Academic Research, https://doi.org/10.1007/978-3-031-48147-5_2

a chat:	a series of exchanges with a chatbot
coax:	persuade/encourage the bot to provide you with a more suitable output
crafting:	the art of writing an effective prompt to succinctly request a bot to respond with optimal output
flip:	change the order, typically the order of the key words in the prompt
framing:	how the context is defined, and how the instructions to the bot are worded
interactor:	for the purposes of this chapter, the person who writes a prompt in order to interact with a chatbot
iterate:	repeat the prompt but using different words and adding more detail
meta prompt:	an instruction to take your prompt and improve it
negative prompt:	tells a bot what response you are NOT looking for. This would be included in the main prompt
regenerate:	gets the bot to provide a different response without you writing a new prompt
response:	the output produced by a bot in response to a prompt; in some cases also called a 'result'
style/tone/voice:	how you want your text to sound (e.g. serious, light-hearted, academic)
tailor:	personalize to your specific case
tweak:	improve your prompt by making fine adjustments to it; also known as 'fine tuning'

In academic English, you are likely to use a prompt to:

- ask a question
- generate a text
- check a text written by you
- translate a text

On the basis of the bot's output, you may need to tweak the prompt in order to coax it to produce something closer to what you had in mind. Just as you have learned how to conduct more and more accurate searches on, for example, Google, you need to learn how to produce more effective prompts.

Much research has been carried out on how to generate prompts to get a specific image, to write marketing literature for companies, to help IT developers write code, and so on. There are now even online marketplaces where prompts that have been verified as getting good results are bought and sold. However, little has been written to help you as a non-native researcher to achieve a successful outcome with a bot. And most of what has been written has focused on generating new text, rather than the equally important task of correcting and improving an existing text that you have written.

This book covers both tasks.

2.3 Thinking about how to write a prompt

Using a bot to find answers, generate emails, prepare presentation scripts, and correct your English will save you a lot of time. Some of this time saved is well worth spending on crafting your **PROMPT**. Before composing your prompt, think about what you want the bot to do (answer a question, generate a text, translate a text, correct a text), what key words would be useful for the bot, and whether you want the response to be written in a particular style.

You should also tell the bot:

- what the context is - the main topic, plus the key subtopic/s of interest to you
- what your aim is - what outcome you want, whether you intend using it for a specific audience
- why it is important for you
- what level of detail you want
- the length of the text that you want the bot to write for you

At the time of writing, chatbots are still in their early stages. AI bots currently lack the judgement and common sense of a human being. It helps if you imagine the bot as having access to a wealth of information, but not knowing by default what it exactly you want.

See the bot as a beginner in your area of expertise. So don't

- use any confusing or ambiguous language or terms
- make assumptions that someone new to your field would not understand
- avoid jargon that could be applied to any field, focus on words that are specific to your field

Be as specific as possible when writing your **PROMPT**.

Poor: **Please correct this abstract.**

Better: **Please correct the English of this abstract on marine biology.**

Best: **Please correct the English of this abstract on marine biology, specifically the analysis of environmental DNA (eDNA), for a paper entitled 'xyz'. Do NOT change the order of the sentences. Do NOT change any technical terms.**

If you have some text for the bot to work on, put the text in "inverted commas" at the end of the **PROMPT**. Alternatively, end the **PROMPT** with a colon (:). For example:

Correct this abstract: "In this paper we blah blah blah blah."

Correct this abstract: In this paper we blah blah blah blah.

In any case, the bot will likely understand where the prompt ends and the text begins.

You can also use a bot to find some information, as in the example below.

Poor: **What is the internet of things?**

Better: **Summarize the key concepts of the internet of things.**

Much better: **Summarize three key concepts of the internet of things. Use three separate paragraphs. Do NOT use bullet points. Ensure there is a logical transition from one paragraph to the next. Do NOT provide a concluding paragraph.**

Note how in the 'much better' **PROMPT** I have told the bot what I do NOT want it to do.

The bot will not necessarily respect your instructions. Some part of the skills needed to write an effective **PROMPT** are similar to those for writing a secure password – the less generic the better. The rest of this chapter deals with how to write non-generic prompts.

2.4 Length of prompt, action verbs, word order, vocabulary

How long and complex should a **PROMPT** be? If you ask a bot this question, it will tell you: (i) to avoid excessive length or unnecessary information, and that (ii) a series of concise instructions within the same **PROMPT** are easier for the model to interpret and generate accurate responses.

In my experience four to five short sentences of up to ten words each seems to produce good results.

You obviously want to include technical words in your **PROMPT** that are relevant to your field.

However, if you want the bot to generate a text, you also need non-key words, such as verbs of action:

act like	counter	focus	predict
analyze	create	formulate	propose
answer	describe	generate	provide
apply	demonstrate	give	rank
argue for/against	detail	highlight	recommend
assess	devise	identify	search for
be (take role of)	discuss	illustrate	suggest
calculate	elaborate	interpret	validate
comment	evaluate	invent	write
compare	explain	justify	
contrast	find	list	

The verbs above should give you ideas on how to formulate your prompt so that the bot does exactly what you want it to do. Here are a lot of examples to show you the incredible variety of prompts beginning with an action verb that you can give a bot.

Analyze the effects of regular exercise on preventing Alzheimer's.

Compare the rationale given for adopting a vegan diet presented in these texts.

Demonstrate the best way to wire an electric plug in China.

Extract the three main keywords from this abstract that I can use in a similar abstract.

Find three case studies on poverty in the global north. Where possible, list the author, title, and journal.

Generate a question that will elicit accurate responses from the right experts on Quora. The question should be based on the following information:

Identify five experts on xyz who I could invite to our conference on xyz.

Imagine you are my professor. Comment on this text that I have written. Focus more on the negative than the positive.

List some generic phrases that I can use in a conclusions section of a paper.

Propose a way to exploit the waste products of the construction industry.

Provide statistics with references that support the need to raise the minimum wage.

Rank the top five papers on the negative effects of climate change.

Suggest 10 FAQs on the topic of brain tumors.

Use bullets to list the five main take home points using this script for a PowerPoint presentation.

Validate the methods used in the three methods sections that I will insert one by one after this prompt. The method of validation should include x, y and z.

Changing the order of the words in the **PROMPT**, will also affect the answer. Compare these two **PROMPT**s:

Analyze the effects of regular exercise on preventing Alzheimer's.

Explain how Alzheimer's can be prevented through regular exercise.

The first **PROMPT** generated 411 words with a total of five paragraphs. No bullets. The second **PROMPT** generated 450 words, with seven paragraphs. The middle five paragraphs were bulleted. The two texts also differed in terms of content, i.e. some factors regarding exercise were unique to one response. Both texts were useful in different ways, one was not clearly better than the other.

So it is worth:

- changing the **PROMPT** and comparing the output (you might want to use bits from both)
- pressing 'regenerate response'- again comparing the output

Instead, if you want the bot to check the English of a text that you have already written or to translate it, then you will need other verbs:

> check/check for, correct, critique, edit, expand, paraphrase, proofread, revise, rewrite, shorten, suggest alternatives/variations, summarize

See 2.5 to learn how to use these verbs within a **PROMPT**.

2.5 Don't overload your prompt with too many details: divide into sub-prompts

If you have ever tried creating an AI image, you will know that a typical prompt can contain a massive amount of details, even up to 15 items of information!

Chatbots cannot cope with that level of detail. The following prompt is made up of four elements:

> **Paraphrase the entire text, change the examples, retain the bullets but re-order the bullets to get a more logical sequence.**

However in my tests the bot only managed to complete the first of the four tasks of the **PROMPT** above. It needed an extra **PROMPT** to complete the tasks successfully:

> **Could you try again and replace any specific examples given with other examples (so NOT Student's t test but some kind of equivalent).**

2.6 Prompts for correcting your English

Chapter 4 deals with how to check your English using a bot.

Below are some example **PROMPT**s for checking and improving/enhancing your English:

At the beginning of the first **PROMPT** you need to provide some background context before stating the exact task.

> **I am a non-native speaker and an academic. I want to submit my paper on xyz for publication in an international journal named ABC. I will insert a series of texts from this paper. Your task will be the same each time I insert a text. <u>Your task is to correct the English, but NOT to paraphrase or make any unnecessary changes</u>. Is this clear?**

Any further **PROMPT**s you give will all be part of the same chat, so you don't need to repeat the preliminary information about being a non-native speaker, academic, and publication in a journal each time.

However, you do need to repeat the part of the prompt that is <u>underlined</u>. This is because the bot is NOT consistent in the way it modifies a text. It may respect your prompt the first few times you insert a text, but then may start paraphrasing, summarizing, introducing bullet points.

Below are some prompts you can use to get the bot to make specific changes or to identify specific issues. You can use them separately or in combination. However, the more instructions you give within the same prompt, the less likely the bot is to respect all of them.

> **Rewrite the following text using an impersonal passive form / style.**

> **Highlight any grammar errors and suggest corrections.**

> **Highlight any instances of passive voice where it is not clear who or what the subject is.**

> **Check for consistency in punctuation.**

> **Rephrase or break up any sentences longer than 20 words to be more concise and engaging.**

> **Add any words or phrases to make the transition clear from one sentence to the next, and one paragraph to the next.**

Correcting and improving your English, does not just involve grammar and vocabulary, but also tone and style. For example:

Make this sentence more formal/academic.

Transform this technical sentence into an explanation for non-experts.

Rewrite this sentence in an informal/conversational tone.

Adjust the tone of this sentence to fit an academic context.

2.7 Prompts for suggestions for improving your text

The following **PROMPT**s all begin with '**Suggest** ...' and end with '**Do not make any changes to the text. Just list your suggestions'.** The idea is that the bot is not going to correct your text, but only list possible improvements.

alternative vocabulary choices to improve readability, and alternative sentence constructions for greater variety.

alternatives for any phrases and non-key words that are repeated more than twice

alternatives to any jargon

how to rewrite this complex sentence in everyday language that a non-expert could understand

how to improve transitions between paragraphs

how to make my text more engaging and interactive

how to make this text sound and look more like a text from the following scientific journal [name of journal]

how to restructure the text for greater impact

improvements to my use of tenses to make their usage consistent, i.e. to make sure I always use the same tense for the same function

rephrasings of ambiguous, weak, vague, or unclear language

ways to break up this long paragraph for greater readability

ways to give this text greater impact

ways to make this text sound more academic/scientific/technical

what information is possibly redundant and could be removed

Even if for you your **PROMPT** is really clear (i.e. that you only want suggestions), the bot may still misinterpret the prompt and make corrections rather than suggestions. In such cases, you need to inform the bot:

You misunderstood my prompt. I asked for a suggestion. I did NOT want you to modify my text. Please try again. Only make suggestions.

Other prompts:

Identify any missing information and suggest additions

Expand on this idea in more detail

Elaborate on this sentence to provide more context

Create a more engaging version of this title of a paper

Describe this concept using an imaginative comparison

2.8 How to get a chatbot to paraphrase a text without changing the key words

A common worry when using a chatbot is that it may remove or paraphrase key words that you absolutely want to keep. With Grammarly and QuillBot this is less of an issue as they both automatically visualize the changes they have made. To prevent the chatbots from removing key words without you being aware put your key words into capital letters. Many bots lose most formatting (e.g. italics, bold, different font types) when you insert a text. However, chatbots tend not automatically convert UPPER CASE letters into lower case. Here is a procedure that you can follow.

Before inserting your text into the bot's windows, highlight all the words in your document that you do NOT want the bot to change, as in the screenshot below.

Simple does not mean primitive. The text may have a complex idea, and you can use terms and introduce complex concepts. But if a thought can be expressed simply, it must not be complicated. Even if you write for scientists. Even if your reader is a government official or an academic. There is not a single situation where it is best to express something in difficult language, when it could be expressed in simple language.

Then from the Format menu, select 'Font', then into 'All caps'.

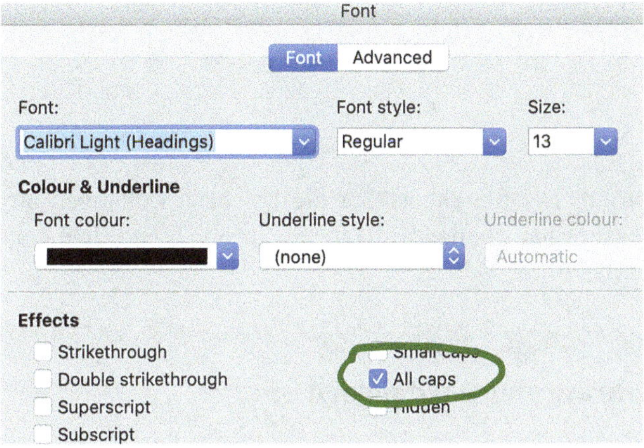

This will produce a text that looks like this.

SIMPLE DOES NOT MEAN PRIMITIVE. The text may have a COMPLEX idea, and you can use terms and introduce complex concepts. But if a thought can be expressed simply, it must not be COMPLICATED. Even if you write for SCIENTISTS. Even if your reader is a GOVERNMENT OFFICIAL or an ACADEMIC. There is not a single situation where it is best to express something in DIFFICULT LANGUAGE, when it could be expressed in SIMPLE LANGUAGE.

You then insert the text above into the bot's window. Use the following **PROMPT**:

> **Please paraphrase the following text. Do not change any of the words in CAPITAL LETTERS.**

You may find that the **PROMPT** does not work. So you have to give a further **PROMPT**:

> **Sorry, but you changed the words in CAPITAL LETTERS. Please repeat, but do NOT change the words in CAPITAL LETTERS.**

This should then generate a response like the one in the screenshot below.

> "SIMPLE DOES NOT IMPLY PRIMITIVE. The text may have a COMPLEX idea, and you can use terms and introduce complex concepts. But if a thought can be expressed simply, it must not be COMPLICATED. Even if you write for SCIENTISTS. Even if your reader is a GOVERNMENT OFFICIAL or an ACADEMIC. There is not a single situation where it is best to express something in DIFFICULT LANGUAGE when it could be expressed in SIMPLE LANGUAGE."

Examine the bot's output. Double check that the bot hasn't changed any words (in the above case it has changed 'mean' to 'imply'), and then continue inserting your texts.

2.9 How to paraphrase and avoid plagiarism

As an academic, you CANNOT:

- take a sentence / paragraph written by another author
- get a bot to paraphrase this sentence / paragraph
- cut and paste it into your own paper without acknowledging the author

Equally you cannot do the same with something you have written elsewhere and which has already been published. This is known as self-plagiarism.

So if you ask a bot to paraphrase an existing text (already published by you or another author), you need to specify this in your **PROMPT**. For example,

> **The following text has already been published in Wallwork, AI-assisted Writing and Presenting in English, Springer (2024). I would like you to paraphrase it, but acknowledge Wallwork:**

The bot will then paraphrase using one of the following forms of acknowledgement:

> *According to Wallwork (2024), writing in short simple sentences is good style.*
>
> *Writing in short simple sentences is good style (Wallwork, 2024).*
>
> *What is considered good writing style in different languages and countries generally involves long complex sentences with are writer-focused rather than reader-focused. However, as Wallwork (2024) points out, a simple style is often preferable.*

In summary, if you do decide to use the paraphrasing options offered by AI, it is essential that you acknowledge and reference the source of whatever you have paraphrased. Not to do so is unethical and could damage your reputation.

To learn more about the issues involved in plagiarism see Chapter 11 in *English for Writing Research Papers* (editions before 2023).

2.10 How to submit an entire document to a chatbot for correction

Unless you use a browser extension, it is currently possible to submit an entire document to the free version of a chatbot. You can only submit around 450 words at a time (ChatGPT) or 2000 characters (Copilot).

However, with Curie you can submit an entire document. Remember, however, that although Curie is generally effective in correcting your English, there are a number of essential areas listed in 1.3–1.4, where it does not flag some key mistakes. Note: At the time of writing this book, AJE's tool Curie was not available: with this very useful tool you can upload an entire paper and have it corrected in Track Changes. I plan to cover Curie in a future book.

If you want the free version of a chatbot to correct an entire document, you may find the following procedure to be useful:

1. Open a 'New chat'.
2. Give the bot the following prompt.

   I am submitting a paper on ABC to the Journal of XYZ. I want you to correct my English. I do NOT want you to paraphrase or summarize my text. I do NOT want you to change any technical terms. I will be submitting a series of texts. Before I do, please confirm that you have understood my prompt.

3. The bot will then confirm that it has understood and will 'do my best to assist you with English corrections while adhering to your guidelines'.
4. You cannot submit more than about 450 words at a time. Submit chunks of text, preferably paragraphs. (Note: My tests revealed that 450 words seems to be the max, however ChatGPT itself recommends 100-150 words at a time)
5. Keep doing this until you have submitted the entire text.
6. Copy your entire chat and paste it into a Word file, and name the file 'Chat'.
7. Delete all the parts of the text containing any prompts or which are your original text. You are aiming to create a text that only contains the bot's revised texts.
8. Use the 'Clear formatting' feature of Word (under 'Edit), this will remove all the grey background.
9. Then use the 'Compare documents' feature of Word. Upload your original file and the Chat file.
10. Word will generate a new document where you can see in Track Changes the differences between your original and the Chat. You will not necessarily see where Chat has changed the formatting (Chat removes all bold and italics).
11. If your original document does not contain much formatting, I suggest you work on the Chat file (i.e. use it as a master file), and focus on the phrases that you do NOT want to accept (i.e. that you want to reject). Reject these words and phrases. Then highlight the entire document and 'Accept All Changes'.
12. As an alternative to Point 11, and in order to retain the formatting of your original file, use your original file as the master file and correct it using the 'good' changes from the Chat file.
13. Re-read the entire document again.

Bots are NOT consistent in following instructions. Check very carefully that the bot has been correcting rather than summarizing. Particularly with captions for figures and tables, ChatGPT sometimes summarizes the info contained in the caption, rather than correcting it.

Also, remember that a bot **CANNOT** perform certain vital tasks – see 1.4 for a list of things a bot cannot do.

Chapter 3
Pre-editing

3.1 Introduction

Pre-editing means making modifications to your text so that you stand a greater chance of a machine translator or chatbot accurately rendering your text in English.

This chapter tells you how to pre-edit your text either for subsequent:

- editing via ChatGPT (or similar) if the text is written in English
- translation via Google Translate (or similar) if the text is written in your native language

The pre-editing suggestions made in this chapter include the ten points mentioned below. Currently machine translation and chatbots **CANNOT** automatically help you with such issues.

1. Divide lengthy sentences into shorter ones.
2. Rearrange the word order to reflect English syntax.
3. Eliminate redundancy.
4. Don't use synonyms for keywords.
5. Be careful with ambiguity and gender issues with pronouns.
6. Using active rather than sentences usually leads to fewer mistranslations.
7. Avoid ambiguity caused by nouns that are countable in your language but not in English.
8. Avoid ambiguity with the gerund.
9. Use specific and active words instead of vague ones.
10. Use English punctuation conventions.

A. Wallwork, *AI-Assisted Writing and Presenting in English*, English for Academic Research, https://doi.org/10.1007/978-3-031-48147-5_3

Making the above changes to your text in your own language is much easier than making them to a text that is already in English. You obviously have much more control over your own language. So the above ten changes are particularly useful if you are submitting a text to machine translation. They are also useful if you want to improve a text that you have already written in English and which you intend to then submit to a chatbot to correct any errors in English usage.

3.2 Checking for basic inaccuracies that are not specifically English language related

Before submitting a text to translation into English, you need to check that the version in your own language doesn't contain mistakes. The seven points listed below are not language dependent – they could be made in your language, in the English language, or any other language.

If such inaccuracies are contained in a text in your own language, this will be reflected in the output of a machine translator. On the other hand, if they are contained in a text that you have written directly in English, a chatbot may resolve some (but not all) of them.

You need to ensure that

1. there is no multiple repetition of non-key words, such as using "innovative" several times in a paragraph.
2. you use an initial capital letter for certain words when necessary, such as "World Health Organization"
3. there is grammatical agreement between subject and verb; for example, "She writes" instead of "She write."
4. the entire text uses the same level of formality
5. all words are spelled correctly; for instance, "responsible" instead of "responsable", "career" instead of "carrier"; and that nowords areattachedtogether.
6. accents are used correctly; for instance, "déjà vu" instead of "deja vu," and use the appropriate character with the accent as needed.
7. punctuation is correct. For instance, note the difference between these two sentences: Woman: "*Without her, man is nothing*" vs. "*Woman, without her man, is nothing*".

3.3 You can submit a text with a mix of English and your own language to machine translation

You can submit a text to Google Translate that is a mixture of your own language and English. So to avoid an automatic translator mistranslating the key words from your field, it is a good idea to write them directly in English, even if the rest of the text is in your own language.

3.4 Making a text English-ready

'English ready' means that a text you have written in your own language has been modified to make it adhere to the rules of good writing in English.

In all the examples in the sections below you will first see the original sentence, followed by the English-ready sentence. Imagine that the original sentence was either written in the writer's mother tongue or was written by the writer directly in English but following the writing style of the author's own language.

3.5 Divide lengthy sentences into shorter ones

The longer your sentence, the greater the chance it will be (i) mistranslated when you use automatic translation, (ii) misunderstood by your readers.

Below is an example:

ONE LONG SENTENCE *Even if the occurrence of this particular form of pulmonary tumor occurs on a rare basis, since the behavior of these tumors is extremely difficult to predict and the histological features resembling a discrete cell tumor may lead to misdiagnose a C2 tumor as a C1 tumor, it would be of interest to characterize those lesions and to take them into account in the differential diagnosis of hereditary or congenital tumors.*

ENGLISH-READY (THREE SHORT SENTENCES) *This form of pulmonary tumor is extremely rare and its behavior is extremely difficult to predict. The histological features, which resemble a discrete cell tumor, may mean that a C2 tumor is misdiagnosed as a C1 tumor. It would thus be interesting to characterize these lesions and to take them into account in the differential diagnosis of hereditary or congenital tumors.*

3.6 Rearrange the word order to reflect English syntax: subject + verb + object (all three parts as close as possible without intervening clauses)

You can learn about correct word order in English in Chapter 17 in *English for Academic Research: Grammar, Usage and Style.*

Obviously, you cannot totally adopt English word order in a text written in your own language, but if you can:

1. Put the subject before the verb.
2. Put the object as close after the verb as possible.
3. Keep the subject, verb and object as close to each other as possible – don't insert any intervening phrases.
4. Don't put the key information in the middle of the phrase.

On the other hand, if you are writing directly in English, then you MUST follow the four guidelines above.

3.7 Eliminate redundancy

The more you write, the greater the chance of errors. When you finish writing a paragraph, analyse it and decide what you could delete. When you have completed the whole document, see if there are any sentences, paragraphs or sections that you could delete entirely.

Compare this pair of sentences:

a) The research focused the comparison between the year 2033, when a severe spring frost occurred, and the 2026–2028 period, characterized by a lack of natural spring frosts.

b) We compared 2033, when a severe spring frost occurred, with 2026–2028, when there were no natural spring frosts.

The second version contains 30% fewer words but retains the same information.

In the next pair, the second version is not only shorter but is also more specific.

c) There is a wide variety of studies dealing with the evaluation and the achievement of clarity in technical manuals. We will discuss a certain number of them that in our opinion are of particular interest to our research.

d) Around 20 studies on clarity in technical manuals can be found in the literature [for a review, see refs. 10 and 15]. We discuss three papers that we believe that are most relevant to our research.

If your reader has to search for key information that is hidden in a mass of redundant words then you are forcing them to make an unnecessary effort. Also, if readers find redundancy in the first sentences of a text, they will assume that there is a good chance that the rest of the text also contains redundancy. This means that they will start to read quickly and instead of reading each individual word, they will start to scan, i.e. to read one in five or six words. They will also quickly lose interest.

Everything you write should add value. If you eliminate the unnecessary and try to be precise, your important points will stand out clearly for the reader.

3.8 Don't use synonyms for keywords

Whether you are writing directly in English or in your own language for subsequent machine translation into English, never use synonyms for <u>key</u> words.

A non-key word is like the ones given below, which are interchangeable with no or very little difference in meaning:

Figure 3 shows that ...

Figure 3 highlights ...

Figure 3 reports that ...

Using different words simply gives variety to your text. The reader is not wondering whether there is any difference between *report* and *shows*.

On the other hand, key words tend to be nouns and tend to be words that give the most meaning to the text.

Below are three sentences that begin three consecutive paragraphs in a paper on corporate taxation:

> *Companies have to pay many taxes.*
> *In fact, occasionally enterprises fail because of over-taxation.*
>
> *Some firms resolve this problem by moving their headquarters to countries where the tax rate is lower.*

The three words underlined are key words in the field of corporate taxation. However, the author was using them as synonyms to create variety for the reader. Instead, the reader may be confused and may wonder what the difference is between *company, enterprise* and *firm*. To avoid this problem, never find synonyms for key words.

If you insist on using synonyms for keywords in your own language, there is a chance that a machine translator may select the wrong word as the English translation, particularly if the same word in your language can have different translations in English.

3.9 Be careful with pronouns – they may be ambiguous

A sentence or phrase is ambiguous or vague when it has more than one interpretation or its interpretation is not obvious. If your language has gender (masculine, feminine, neuter), when you use a pronoun it may be clear what the pronoun refers to because it is the same gender as the preceding noun. Unfortunately a phrase that has no ambiguity in your language, when translated into English can become ambiguous.

Be very careful when you use pronouns (*this, that, them, it* etc) – make sure it is clear what they refer to and don't be afraid of repeating the same noun many times rather than using a pronoun.

Can you see where the ambiguity might be in these phrases?

> *Sarah told Amy that she had passed the exam.*
>
> *The students handed in their assignments, and the teacher praised them.*
>
> *The shoe brands (e.g. Adidas, Vans, Reebok) want the leather producers to move towards environmental sustainability. However, they are not fully convinced about reusing materials in the productive processes of the leather.*

It's unclear whether "she" refers to Sarah or Amy, "them" refers to the students or the assignments, and "they" to the brands (i.e. the companies that sell shoes) or the leather producers.

To enhance clarity and avoid ambiguity, it's important to ensure that the antecedent (the word the pronoun refers to) is clearly identified and unambiguous in the context. If there's potential for confusion, consider rephrasing the sentence or explicitly stating the antecedent again to provide clarity to the reader.

3.10 Using active sentences usually leads to fewer mistranslations

The following sentence is not clear.

> *The problem of dishonesty among politicians was investigated through a case study.*

The reader cannot tell who did the investigation, you or someone else. So a better solution, when you (i.e. you and your research group) are the subject of the verb, is to write.

> *Through a case study, we investigated the problem of dishonesty among politicians.*

You could argue that the reader will know from the context whether you have done something or whether it has been done by someone else. Not necessarily. You cannot control what the reader reads. They may read your sentence in isolation. They may read it before they have read about the context. You simply don't know. So you can massively increase your chances of being understood if you use an active sentence, where you are obliged to put the subject of the verb.

Clearly, there are exceptions to this, for example the Methods section in a paper, or when you are writing a technical description. In any case, when writing about methods and results, always establish at the beginning of a paragraph who is the subject of the verbs used in the rest of the paragraph.

3.11 Ambiguity caused by nouns that are countable in your language but not in English

Many words that may be countable in your language are uncountable in English. For example, *information* is singular in English. You cannot say *informations*, *many information* etc, nor can you the pronouns *they/them* to refer back to *information*. This means that the following sentence could be confusing.

> *Since such information is relatively easily available, little can be done to prevent an adversary from obtaining them. They are also held in several different databases.*

A native English speaking reader will not connect *they* and *them* to *information*. And if written in your own language, then Google Translate will not understand what *they* and *them* refer to. Moreover, a chatbot will not be able to correct the sentence.

Other nouns that are uncountable in English, but may be countable in your language are: *access, accommodation, advertising, advice, agriculture* (and other subjects of study), *capital, cancer* (and other diseases and illnesses), *consent, electricity* (and other intangibles), *English* (and other languages), *equipment, evidence, expertise, feedback, functionality, furniture, gold* (and other metals), *hardware, health, industry, inflation, intelligence, luck, know-how, machinery, money, news, oxygen* (and other gases), *personnel, poverty, progress, research, safety, security, software, staff, storage, traffic, training, transport, waste, wealth, welfare, wildlife.*

So what can you do? If you are aware that a word that you have written in your own language in its plural form is uncountable in English, then it is worth writing that word in its singular form and using singular pronouns when referring back to it.

Obviously, you may not know the rule or may not have thought about this issue while you are writing. So an alternative is to check the English output. Check that:

- it is clear what all the pronouns refer back to
- the pronouns are in the correct form (i.e. singular or plural depending on whether the noun they refer to is singular or plural, respectively)
- consider substituting pronouns with the noun that they refer to. This means that an automatic translator cannot make a mistake, and the reader can be 100% sure of the meaning.

You may think this is a minor issue. It is not. Most papers will have sentences where there are two possible meanings and this can lead to confusion for the referee, editors and readers.

For details on the use of countable and uncountable nouns see Chapter 9 in *English for Academic Research: Grammar, Usage and Style.*

3.12 Avoiding ambiguity with the gerund (*-ing* form)

In the following sentence, Anna is the subject of both verbs (*teach, have*), so it's not clear who has a good level of English: Anna or the students.

> *Anna teaches the students having a good level of English.*

So, consider replacing *-ing* with a different form.

> *Anna teaches the/those students that have a good level of English.*
>
> *Anna teaches the students since she has a good level of English.*

The problem with the *-ing* form is that it is not immediately clear who or what the subject is. Here is another example:

> *Swimming in the ocean, dolphins were seen by the tourists.*

Who is swimming dolphins or tourists?

A bot is unlikely to be able to help you identify ambiguity in your sentences. This is something that you have to do. However, it is really difficult for us to spot our own errors in writing. The problem is that we read what we THINK we have written, rather than what is actually on the page.

> If you have a paragraph that you think is particularly important and which you want your readers to interpret in only one way, then you need the help of a qualified native English speaker – using a chatbot is NOT enough.

3.13 Use specific words instead of vague ones

Look at the phrases below. The underlined words (primarily adjectives and adverbs) are vague. Would you, as a reader, be able to say what they really mean?

> *The research project spanned a relatively short timeframe, yielding significant findings that will have a precise impact.*
>
> *The forested area exhibited a somewhat substantial growth of flora and fauna, with an important amount of diversity.*
>
> *The company's expansion strategy has led to an adequate growth in the last few decades, transforming it into a reasonably strong player in the field.*
>
> *Participants performed quite effectively, and in a number of cases their outcomes were notable compared to their counterparts.*
>
> *We applied a proper strategy for the calculation.*

A common mistake is to assume your readers will automatically understand what you have written. This is because you as the author know your topic extremely well, in fact you may have been working on it for several months, even years. This means that you may use words and expressions which to you are clear, but to the reader may not be. In reality the reader cannot know what *relatively short timeframe*, *precise impact*, *adequate growth* etc mean.

Such vague words and phrases must be replaced both when writing in your own language and in English.

3.14 Avoid *he*, *he/she*

Both when writing in your own language (for subsequent translation into English) and directly in English, never use a masculine pronoun to refer to a generic person.

> *No! When choosing a new doctor, make sure* he *is qualified.*
>
> *Yes! When choosing a new doctor, make sure* they *are qualified.*

In modern English it does not matter that *doctor* is singular and *they* is plural.

To ensure that Google Translate makes correct interpretations, when writing in your own language never use a singular pronoun (including *he/she*) when you could use a plural one. This obviously means changing a singular subject to a plural subject.

> No! *The reader can find further information if* he *consults xyz.*
>
> No! *The reader can find further information if* he/she *consults xyz.*
>
> Yes! *Readers can find further information if* they *consult xyz.*

Some languages don't require a subject before a verb. This leaves the decision to the automatic translator as to whether *he*, *she* or *they* is required. It is thus always better to insert the subject or pronoun, and in the case of a personal pronoun, where possible to use third person plural (*they*).

3.15 Use English punctuation conventions

Limit the amount of punctuation you use in a sentence. A sentence should ideally be understandable with very little punctuation. If it needs a lot of punctuation, it probably needs to be restructured in a simple way. In any case:

- Replace semicolons (,) with a period (.); and begin a new sentence.
- Consider deleting phrases that you have put in parentheses. If, instead, the information contained in them is important, then remove the parentheses, and have the phrase in a separate sentence.

Be careful of sentences such as this:

> No! *The two tables below give details of the <u>parameters which</u> are not self-explanatory.*

The reader does not know if the writer means that none of the parameters are self-explanatory – in which case there should be a comma before *which* – or if the table only lists those parameters that need to be explained – in which case which should be replaced with *that.*

The above is just an example of the ambiguity that can be caused by not using punctuation appropriately. Your aim is to write sentences that have only have ONE possible interpretation. So in cases such as the above which require an advanced level of English both on your part and the part of the reader, it is best to simplify the sentence. So in the above case you could write:

> *The two tables below give details of <u>only those parameters that</u> are not self-explanatory.*

3.16 Being self-critical and knowing when to enlist a human's help

Pre-editing entails being self-critical (see 6.5). You need to learn how to look at what you have written and think about how to improve the readability. You can boost the level of interest by:

1. using fewer words by removing all redundancy
2. dividing up long sentences
3. adding concrete details and examples
4. highlighting the importance of your findings, and differentiating between what you found and what others found

These four points, not just the grammatical accuracy of your English, will determine whether a journal decides to accept your paper or not. You need to take them into account whether you write in your own language or directly in English.

It is much easier for you to make such changes when you have a version of your paper written in your own language. I suggest that you experiment with writing your papers in your native language and not in English. In this way, you have much more control over the final output.

In my experience with my own PhD students, Google Translate produces a better translation of their work than they are able to do manually. But I need to reiterate that there are many things that a machine translator and a chatbot CANNOT do. These are listed at the beginning of this chapter and also in 1.4. If a paper is really important to you, then I suggest you involve the services of a professional editing agency and get a human to help you where AI cannot help – see Chapter 9.

3.17 Using machine translation can also improve your English

Your main aim in writing a paper is NOT to improve and practise your English. Your main aim is to get your paper published and disseminate your results to the rest of the world.

In any case, in the process you will still learn English by analysing the words and sentences that Google Translate (GT) produces and comparing them with how you might have translated such sentences. The same is true if you submit a text for correction to ChatGPT, you can improve your English by looking at the kinds of changes the bot has made (but remembering the bot is NOT always right – see 6.6).

You will also be more motivated to find the mistakes that GT has made than you would be if you had written directly in English. In fact, it is easier to spot the mistakes made by another 'person' (in this case GT) than the mistakes that we make ourselves.

Chapter 4
Using a chatbot as a language editor to check your English

4.1 Introduction

Below is a summary of some of the points regarding the editing skills chatbots: see 1.2–1.4 for more details.

THINGS IT DOES WELL

- Corrects grammar mistakes
- Identifies where punctuation needs adding
- Paraphrases and summarizes
- Makes suggestions on improving content and style of your text
- Make phrases more concise
- Transforms passive to active sentences

AREAS WHERE IT MAY HAVE PROBLEMS

- Implements too many changes
- Makes illogical connections between paragraphs
- Doesn't follow the prompt
- Generates generic phrases
- Doesn't reduce text by specified number of words
- Sentences always similar length – no variation
- Always uses same structure when generating text

THINGS IT IS CURRENTLY UNABLE TO DO

- List all changes made – it just lists some.
- Only make 'essential' changes
- Identify ambiguity
- Warn about biased or non-gender neutral language
- Make your key findings stand out
- Tell you that you have written too much
- Hedge
- Warn about plagiarism or potential negative comments by referees

A. Wallwork, *AI-Assisted Writing and Presenting in English*, English for Academic Research, https://doi.org/10.1007/978-3-031-48147-5_4

Chatbots are NOT a perfect editing tool, but they can certainly improve the accuracy of your English.

To learn what prompts to use see Chapter 2.

In Section 4.2 you will see that you cannot use a machine translator to check your English. In fact, this chapter focuses on using ChatGPT (but refers equally well to other bots such as Copilot and Gemini, and generally also to Curie). You can find details of how to use machine translators in Chapter 3 and Chapter 10.

In Sections 4.3–4.7 you will learn how to use ChatGPT to edit the English of your written texts. You will also discover the areas where a bot does NOT do a good job.

In Sections 4.8–4.12 you will learn how you can use ChatGPT to analyse the content (rather than the English) of what you have written. I focus on two sections of a paper – Titles, Abstracts. If you want to learn what a bot can do in the other sections of a paper, see the following sections in the companion volume *English for Writing Research Papers* (2023 edn.): Introduction 14.10, Review of the Literature 15.9, Methods 16.2, Results 17.9, Discussion 18.12–13, Conclusions 19.3, 19.10.

Section 4.13 looks at other AI editing tools and 4.14 gives an example of how to combine Google Translate and ChatGPT to create an accurate text in English derived from a text written originally in your own language.

4.2 Do NOT use automatic translation software to check your English

If you write something directly into English, you may think that you can use Google Translate, DeepL etc to check your English by translating it back into your own language to see if it makes sense. Unfortunately this does NOT work.

When you write in English you are naturally translating directly from your own language. So, if you submit your English text into Google Translate and translate it back into your own language, the translated text in your own language will probably be very good because the structure of your English sentence is based on the structure of the same sentence in your language.

However, this does NOT indicate that your English version is correct. It only indicates that the resulting text in your own language is what you wanted to say in English.

For example, let's imagine you have written a non-grammatical sentence such as *I am here since yesterday*. You have used the simple present (*I am*) because in your language this is the tense you would use. In reality in such cases the correct tense in English is the present perfect, so the sentence should be *I have been here since yesterday.*

If you get Google Translate to translate *I am here since yesterday* into your own language, then Google Translate's translation will probably look correct in your language because it is a literal translation. However, although the translation into your own language is correct, the original English is not correct (it should be: *I have been here*).

This section originally appeared in the companion volume *English for Interacting on Campus* in Chapter 12 Automatic Translation: Pros and Cons, which covers all areas of being a university student in another country: dealing with face-to-face relations with other students and with professors; writing emails to professors; participating in lectures, meetings, workshops, study groups, seminars etc; socializing both on and off campus; making telephone calls; and understanding native speakers, pronunciation, listening skills, and translation.

4.3 Good changes a bot may make when prompted to correct a text

When given the following prompt:

Correct/Revise/Edit the English of this academic text.

a bot will generally make changes that do not affect your intended meaning. The bot may even make the following useful grammatical changes:

- Change the past tense to the present tense where needed, and vice versa.
- Change *that* with *which*, and vice versa
- Switch *a* to *the*, and vice versa
- Use the correct preposition

If you want the bot to visualize the modification it has made, you can instruct it to put any changed words or phrases into bold or capital letters. However, be aware that the bot does not always highlight all the changes it has made. On the other hand, Curie uses Track Changes to show changes.

The bot will also make your sentences flow better internally in relation to the surrounding sentences and generally improve readability. It will generally implement the following useful changes:

- Make connections between the same noun (*x*) mentioned in two successive sentences by using *this x* or *such an x* in the second reference to the noun.
- If an earlier sentence has begun with 'Firstly', GPT will notice when there is no 'secondly' (or equivalent), and will insert 'secondly', 'then', 'subsequently' etc of its own accord.
- Insert 'however' at the beginning of a sentence where the second part of the sentence in some way qualifies or contradicts the first part.
- Find a more appropriate word or phrase, e.g. it might replace *here, following*, *existence*, *generates*, and *dictating* with *in this study, caused by, presence*, *triggers*, and *controlling*.
- Repeat a key word to avoid ambiguity.
- Sort out unnecessary repetitions of non-key words and phrases.
- Avoid beginning two consecutive sentences with a similar expression. Instead it will try to find synonyms, but without creating any ambiguity. However, you must ensure that the bot does NOT use synonyms for your key words.

The points listed above are key elements of clear writing. Given that a bot may not spot them, you need to critically analyze your text and try to make the same kind of changes listed above.

A bot also seems to have very useful proofreading skills. It will often:

- Add the definition of an acronym where appropriate.
- Add commas where necessary.
- Use semicolons appropriately (e.g. in long lists of items to highlight how they are subdivided into smaller groups).

4.4 Rearranging word and phrase order

It is difficult for you as a non-native speaker of English to know if you are writing sentences with the words in the best or standard order. I recommend that before you complete the first paragraph or section of a document, you try the following **PROMPT** with two or three of your sentences:

> **Rearrange this sentence / paragraph to make it flow more logically.**

The bots responses should then reveal to you areas where you might need to improve the word order in your phrases.

In the example below the bot has shifted *in this study* to a more logical position in terms of the standard order of information in a sentence in English.

> Original: *Accordingly, all these samples were identified as XYZs in this study.*
>
> Bot: *Consequently, in this study all these samples were identified as XYZs.*

A bot will also divide up a string of nouns and adjectives. The original version below is again not the standard order in English

> Original: *It helps mitigate internal oxygen decline by promoting anaerobic metabolism.*
>
> Bot: *It helps mitigate the decline in internal oxygen levels and promotes anaerobic metabolism.*

The bot usually does a good job in relocating key words to near the beginning of the sentence (first example below), but not as good as a professional editing agency (second).

> Bot: *It has been demonstrated that starch is vital for plant survival and the induction of ADH and other anaerobic genes under submergence, as it serves as the primary source of sugars for energy production (Smith et al, 2026).*
>
> Human: *Starch is the main source of sugars for energy production. It is essential for plant survival as well as for the induction of ADH and other anaerobic genes under submergence (Smith et al, 2026).*

The human version

- switches the order of the information by putting the main subject (*starch*) at the beginning
- divides the phrase into two parts
- removes a generic phrase that adds no value (*it has been demonstrated that*)

4.5 Reducing text length

Many academic texts are too long. A bot can help you reduce the length and thus increase the readability of your text. This is also useful when you have to comply with a specific word count. For example you may have written an Abstract of 300 words, but the journal only allows 250 words.

Be careful, sometimes bots cut too much.

After a bot has reduced your text, make sure you reinsert any examples or specific cases that the bot may have removed.

Compare these two versions. The human version contains elements (underlined in the text) from the original version submitted to the bot, and which are absolutely necessary.

Bot: *The activation of HRGs is crucial for the survival of plants under extreme environmental conditions, such as flooding events, which negatively impact plant growth and development.*

Human: *Activating HRGs is key for plants to be able to survive under extreme environmental conditions, such as flooding. Such conditions can lead to soil waterlogging, when only the roots are completely under the water level, or submergence where the entire plant is under water. Both conditions negatively affect plant growth and development.*

If a reviewer has instructed you to reduce your paper by 25%, a bot cannot know which parts to reduce. Only you know. For example, if you give a bot the following **PROMPT**:

> **Reduce the word count of this abstract.**

the bot won't necessarily know what you mean by 'reduce', nor where the reducing should take place. In some cases it may simply halve the length of the original text but at the expense of specific examples. Examples are important for two reasons:

- they provide key information
- they make a text much more enjoyable to read – the problem with texts generated or corrected by a bot, is that they tend, unsurprisingly, to sound soulless and generic

So, after a bot has reduced your text, make sure you reinsert any examples or specific cases that the bot may have removed. Check whether it has combined sentences together, but in doing so has deleted some key information.

***

Another way to reduce the word count of your manuscript is to use the bot to show you – at a sentence level – how you could reduce the number of words.

So you insert the usual prompt:

> **Reduce the word count of this text.**

However, given that you have an entire manuscript to work on, and given a bot's tendency to start ignoring prompts after a while (see 4.7), I suggest you only insert a couple of paragraphs from each section of the paper. Next, analyse what kind of reductions the bot has made in each sentence. Then for the rest of your text and try following the same strategies that the bot has used. This method gives you more control over the outcome and is also a very useful skill to learn. You can then resubmit your texts and just get the bot to correct the text:

> **Correct the English grammar and syntax of this text. Do NOT reduce the word count. Do not summarize or paraphrase.**

4.6 Spelling

A bot can also act as an additional spellchecker by making changes that for instance Microsoft Word's editor doesn't find. So it will correct *X relays on Y,* with *X relies on Y*.

At the manuscript stage of this book, my most frequent typos were *then* vs *than*, and *you* vs *your*. Microsoft Word rarely spotted them, though ChatGPT often corrected them. In any case, it is a good idea to keep a note of the typical typos you make and to do a final check to see that you have not made them. This is clearly only a problem when the typo is word that exists, such as *form* instead of *from*; of course all tools will tell you that *fmor* is wrong!

Spellcheckers and bots don't pick up everything. You need to be careful of typos and confusions between words such as: *addition* vs *addiction*, *analyzes* (v.) vs *analyses* (plural of *analysis*), *assess* vs *asses*, *contest* vs *context*, *choose* vs *chose* vs *choice*, *drawn* vs *drown*, *fell* vs *felt*, *filed* vs *filled* vs *field*, *form* vs *from*, *found* vs *founded*, *guaranteeing* vs *guarantying*, *lose* vs *loose*, *rely* vs *relay*, *review* vs *revise*, *than* vs *then*, *there* vs *their*, *three* vs *tree*, *through* vs *trough*, *two* vs *tow*, *underlying* vs *underling*, *use* vs *sue*, *weighed* vs *weighted*, *which* vs *witch*, *with* vs *whit*.

Never forget to spell check your work, and ensure have the correct language settings in ALL parts of the paper. If you have merged together several documents, each of these documents will have its own language and spelling settings. You need to highlight the entire doc and re-set the spelling and language. Resetting the language will avoid also having both US and UK spellings within the same doc (see 2.5 in *Grammar, Usage and Strategies – Intermediate level*).

4.7 Warning! Bots don't always follow your prompts

Chapter 2 deals with the prompts you can use with a chatbot, but the bot may 'forget' or 'ignore' your prompt. For example, even though you prompt the bot to 'correct' your English, sometimes it just summarizes the text you have inserted. Here is an example:

> Original: *Many of the diurnal rhythms in plants are controlled by a central oscillator known as the circadian clock.*
>
> Bot: *The researchers further investigated whether cyclic hypoxia is regulated by the circadian clock or if it results from a drop in internal oxygen levels during the night.*

As you can see, the bot has summarized the sentence instead of correcting it. When you are in a hurry, there is a chance you may not notice this. So it always best to use a specific prompt, which also includes what you do NOT want the bot to do:

> **Please correct the English of this text. Do NOT simply summarize or paraphrase it.**

Use Microsoft Word's 'compare documents' function to ensure that the bot hasn't made such changes. Such changes will be easy to spot in the document that Word generates. If the bot has inadvertently started summarizing rather than correcting, you will see a lot of inserted blue text (where the bot has begun summarizing) followed by a lot of deleted red text (i.e. the text that you actually wanted the bot to correct rather than summarize).

A bot does not know the difference for you between a key word and a non-key word. So a good idea is to tell the bot what words it should not change. For example:

> **Paraphrase the following text. Note that 'migration' is a key word. This is a text about how birds move from one place to another. 'Translocation' is NOT a synonym for 'migration'. So do NOT change any occurrences of 'migration'.**

When the bot returns your text, you can follow up with another prompt:

> **Re-read your text and confirm to me that you have not changed the word 'migration'.**

The problem in the above case is that the word *migration* is used not just for birds and people but also for technologies. In fact on Google Scholar the word 'translocation' is 30 times more common than 'migration'. The bot tends to opt for the most common term used to describe something. This is why it is important i) to provide the context of your text (e.g. birds), and ii) if you have had similar issues before to anticipate them to the bot (*'Translocation' is NOT a synonym for 'migration'*).

> To check that the bot hasn't eliminated anything or made any unwanted changes (e.g. replacing a key word with a different word), you can paste the bot's output into Word (or equivalent) and then do a 'compare documents'. This will reveal all the changes the bot has made.

4.8 Using a chatbot to make recommendations about the title of your paper

The title you write for your paper may not necessarily be the best title possible.

Imagine your field of research is psychology and that you have drafted the following as the title of your paper: *Online communication platforms in the digital age: new challenges for psychoanalysts and patients.*

You can use AI to come up with possibly better alternatives.

Please suggest a title based on this abstract.

I submitted the abstract of the psychology paper (see 4.9 for the text of the abstract) to four bots: ChatGPT (1–2), Poe (3), Bing (4–7), Gemini (8–12),

1. *Adapting Psychotherapy to the Digital Age: Exploring the Impact of Zoom and Communication Platforms on Therapeutic Relationships and Human Interactions Post-COVID-19*
2. *Zooming In on Psychotherapy: Impact, Adaptations, and Ethical Considerations in the Digital Age*
3. *Exploring the Impact of Zoom in Psychotherapy: Shaping Therapeutic Relationships and Ethical Considerations in the Digital Age*

4. *Zooming into Psychotherapy: Exploring the Impact of Communication Platforms on Mental Health Services*
5. *Virtual Healing: Navigating the Shift to Online Psychotherapy in the Wake of COVID-19*
6. *The Digital Couch: Ethical Considerations and Therapeutic Innovations in Online Psychotherapy*
7. *From Face-to-Face to Screen-to-Screen: The Changing Landscape of Psychotherapy in the Digital Age*
8. *The Impact of Remote Therapy on the Client-Therapist Relationship: Three Case Studies*
9. *Barriers and Strategies in Remote Therapy: A Case Study Approach*
10. *Navigating the Ethical Dilemmas of Teletherapy: A Case Study Analysis*
11. *The Future of Mental Health Care: How Remote Therapy Can Transform the Client-Therapist Relationship*
12. *Best Practices and Ethical Guidelines for Teletherapy: A Case Study Perspective*

Your aim is to then analyze the various titles generated and choose the one that is the most appropriate. The final choice of title should be based on three factors:

1. The journal where you want to submit the article. Choose a title that is similar to the ones that typically appear in this journal.
2. The audience. If you have a lay audience (i.e. not a group of experts) or if you are going to use the title for a presentation at a conference where the audience will be made up of people from different disciplines, then titles 2, 4–12 might be more suitable. Titles 2 and 4 are from two different bots but both make use of the double meaning of 'zoom' (the application and the action of focusing) – these are fun titles and likely to attract more attention than the others. For a presentation you could in fact combine two titles. So you would have the zoom-like title first, followed by a more technical explanation underneath.
3. Specificity. Give expert readers the most information possible. Title 1 is probably the most informative.

It makes sense to write your Abstract before you write a title. You can then submit your Abstract (and possibly also the Conclusions) to various bots and then choose the best title.

Note how all the titles generated by the bots use initial capital letters for all of the words except articles, prepositions and conjunctions. Not all journals require this style and just an initial capital letter for the first word and any other proper nouns. In any case, you can easily prompt the bot to:

Rewrite the title using lower case letters where possible.

4.9 Abstracts: Using a bot to check content

The following abstract was criticized by an editor as 'not fulfilling the requirements of an abstract'. Can you understand what 'requirements' it does NOT fulfill?

> TEXT 1 This paper discusses the utilization of communication platforms, specifically Zoom, in psychotherapy and explores how this change in setting impacts on human interactions, particularly in the aftermath of the COVID-19 pandemic. Therapeutic relationships have changed due to remote therapy sessions, as well as factors such as client engagement, confidentiality, and the potential for miscommunication in the absence of non-verbal cues. There are also ethical considerations related to using digital platforms in psychotherapy, including data privacy, informed consent, and the role of technology in maintaining professional boundaries. Mental health professionals have adapted their practices to the virtual environment, exploring innovative approaches and therapeutic techniques that leverage technology to enhance treatment outcomes. This study thus contributes to a deeper understanding of the broader implications of integrating communication platforms such as Zoom into psychotherapy practices. Valuable insights are offered for mental health practitioners, policymakers, and researchers to navigate the evolving landscape of mental health services, ensuring the delivery of effective, ethical, and accessible care in the digital age.

In any cases where you are unable to judge the quality of your own work, you could use something similar to the following prompt:

The following is an abstract from a psychology paper entitled: Online communication platforms in the digital age: new challenges for psycho-analysts and patients. On the basis of what is typically found in an abstract and how an abstract is typically structured, can you tell me what information is missing?

ChatGPT returned the following:

1. Objectives or research questions: The abstract does not clearly state the specific objectives or research questions that the paper aims to address. It mentions reflections on the concept of the *setting in psychoanalysis* and the challenges posed by the *COVID-19 pandemic*, but it does not explicitly state the goals of the study.

2. Methodology: The abstract does not mention the methodology or research approach used in the study.

3. Results: The abstract does not present any specific results or findings from the study. It mentions an attempt to understand the differences between *analysis conducted in person and online*, but it does not provide any conclusions or outcomes.

4. Implications or significance: The abstract does not discuss the broader implications or significance of the study. It does not mention why studying the *changes in the setting of psychoanalysis in the digital age* is important or how it contributes to the field of psychology.

5. Conclusion: The abstract does not provide a clear conclusion or summary of the paper's main findings. It does not state whether the study supports or challenges existing theories or perspectives.

6. Limitations: The abstract does not mention any potential biases or constraints that may affect the interpretation of the results.

ChatGPT is clearly making an attempt to present its advice by using specific examples from the abstract (which I have highlighted in *italics*). The six points above would be useful in any case for judging any abstract that you write in the future.

You can get further information by prompting the bot:

Imagine you are the journal editor, what feedback would you give?

In this case, ChatGPT told me that the abstract needed to

- clearly differentiate itself from previous work in this field
- include 'concrete examples' and refer to the specific case studies used in the research
- provide more specific information about how the study addresses and explores these ethical issues

- mention any proposed solutions or best practices for maintaining ethical standards in the virtual environment
- provide clear examples of the insights or discoveries that this research brings to the field of psychotherapy

A human editor would be able to tell you that you need to start again and to say what you found, what it means, and to use some specific examples.

So far I have mentioned the very useful recommendations that a bot can make. However, it CANNOT tell you that, for instance, that 110 words of your 190-word Abstract are background information and that most of the content would be more suitable in the Introduction.

Below is a version of the main part of the abstract rewritten by the author upon the suggestions of a professional editing agency. The new texts highlights what I mean by 'specific examples' (in italics) of what was carried out during the research.

TEXT 2 The study presents three case studies to investigate how a new clinical setting – remote therapy sessions conducted via Zoom – has impacted on the client-therapist relationship. *In the first case, we show how an 8-year relationship underwent a significant negative change after transitioning to via Zoom. The physical distance and the client's lack of digital skills led to subtle changes in the dynamics, affecting the client's comfort level and willingness to open up emotionally. In the second, we report a 20-year-old woman's struggle with engagement during virtual therapy sessions due to distractions in the home caused by intrusions by family members. In the third, a clinical vignette showcases an instance where a 25-year-old university student with a poor internet connection suffered the absence of non-verbal cues, leading to misunderstanding and lack of trust, followed by anger.* Through these three cases studies, the study explores the potential barriers that both analysts and clients may face in remote therapy and discusses *strategies to enhance client engagement* and motivation despite the digital setting. The study also examines how mental health practitioners navigate the ethical dilemmas surrounding data privacy when using communication platforms like Zoom. It includes specific measures (*passwords, encryption, no recordings permitted, secure file sharing*) taken by therapists to secure client data and maintain confidentiality, ensuring that the research contributes to the development of best practices and ethical guidelines for teletherapy.

4.10 Abstracts: Using a bot to check content in your own language

If you decide to write your paper directly in your own language (see Chapter 3), then you could insert prompts in your own languages into ChatGPT. I inserted the original Italian version of Text 1 into poe.com/ChatGPT and gave it the same prompt but in Italian. The bot's answer in Italian informed me that the abstract matched the requirements of a journal. The bot was not in any way critical – no mention of the missing aspects.

I then tried a new prompt informing the bot that the abstract had, in fact, been criticized by the editor and to give me advice on how I could improve the abstract. The bot then gave an answer using seven different headings (below is the translation from Italian into English).

Could you translate into English what you have just written in Italian.

Certainly! Here's the translation of the advice I provided:

1. Specificity of the topic: Provide more details about the use of communication platforms in psychotherapy. For example, specifically mention how Zoom is used to conduct remote therapy sessions.
2. Clarity about the scope of the article: Be more explicit about the main objective of the article. For instance, state that the article aims to examine the impact of remote therapy sessions on the quality of therapeutic relationships.
3. References to theoretical background: Integrate key theories or concepts that support your study into the abstract. For example, briefly mention attachment theory or communication theory to emphasize the importance of human interactions in therapy.
4. Highlight key findings or conclusions: Provide an overview of the main results or conclusions of your study. For example, mention that your study identified significant changes in therapeutic relationships following the use of digital platforms like Zoom.
5. Emphasize impact and relevance: Highlight the importance of your findings for the scientific community and professionals in the field. For example, mention that your study provides valuable guidelines for ensuring effective, ethical, and accessible care in the context of online therapy.
6. Avoid including unnecessary details: Strive to keep the abstract concise and focused on the essentials. Remove any information that is not directly relevant to the main topic.
7. Review language and structure: Ensure that the abstract is written clearly, coherently, and well-structured. Use concise and unambiguous sentences, avoiding overly technical or complex language.

As you can see these seven points emphasize different aspects from the six provided by ChatGPT (see 4.9). But they are still to some extent useful but likely reflect the Italian approach to writing a 'good' abstract.

In fact, a bot will do most of its trawling on the internet looking for texts in the language of the prompt given to it, though it may also draw on additional texts in English if necessary. Consequently there is a good chance that asking a bot for advice in your own language, will return advice that will apply to the academic culture of the speakers of your language, e.g. Italians may be more focused on setting the background context than on focusing on the results. This could be useful as it will highlight how academics approach writing in your language, and you can then compare that with the advice that the bot gives in a response to a prompt in English (see also 5.4).

4.11 When writing a paper, start with the Abstract

There is a strong case for writing your Abstract first, i.e. before the rest of the paper, rather than last. This is because ChatGPT can tell you what things you may have not mentioned. If these points are missing from the abstract, it is likely that they are missing, at least partially, in the rest of the paper.

In fact it is a common problem in papers that the author:

1. does not clearly state the specific objectives or research questions that the paper aims to address
2. does not provide any conclusions or outcomes
3. does not state whether the study supports or challenges existing theories or perspectives

Knowing in advance that these three points are crucial, will certainly help you when you write the rest of your paper.

In the past, you may have had a paper accepted for publication that failed to provide the information that a well-written paper would require. Unfortunately, some journal editors and referees themselves tend to focus on the scientific content and the accuracy of the English: they rarely comment on the information that is missing, or on whether a part of the paper is poorly structured.

However, your ultimate aim should be to enable your readers to understand i) why you did something, ii) what you did, iii) how you did it, iv) what the implications were. If readers understand these points, they are then more likely to cite your paper in their paper. If your paper is never cited then there probably wasn't much point in writing and publishing it.

4.12 Ambiguity – a bot CANNOT clarify who did what or who is to do what

You can use a bot to create a perfect text in English, but that does not mean that text is clear. One key skill of writing any kind of document is to make it clear to the reader / audience. For example

- ACADEMIC PAPER Did you carry out 'the survey', 'the investigation', 'the study' or someone else? Was it you who found something or did someone else in the literature find it?
- EMAIL When you give instructions or request information, the recipient needs to know whether they or someone else is expected to do something, by what date/time a request has to be fulfilled etc
- PRESENTATION A good presentation should end with a call to action – see Chapter 10 in *Giving and Academic Presentation in English*). The audience need to know exactly what you want them to do.

Here is an extract from a paper. Read it and see if you can answer the questions that follow.

> During a 30-minute commute, passengers occupying train compartments were observed to allocate an average of 25 minutes engaging in activities such as phone conversations, text messaging, and video viewing. A mere 2% of travelers engaged in conversations with fellow passengers, typically limited to brief interactions such as saying 'sorry' for accidently touching someone or inquiring about seat availability. This stands in stark contrast to a study conducted in 1979 along the same train route. In the late 1970s cell phones did not exist, and the investigation revealed that approximately 68% of passengers engaged in substantive discussions lasting 10 minutes or more. Notably, conversations predominantly occurred between women and women, or men and women. Interestingly, dialogues between two male passengers were also uncommon on the Altrincham-Manchester route.

In each question listed below is the answer a) the author of the text b) someone else?

1. Who found the data regarding the 25 minutes talking?
2. Who conducted the 1979 research?
3. Who conducted the Altrincham / Manchester study?

The problem is that in all three cases the reader cannot be sure if it is the author or someone else.

If the referees who review your paper cannot be sure of the answers above, they will have difficulty in:

- identifying the essence of your contribution
- determining the degree of utility of your contribution
- judging whether your contribution merits publication

This is something AI cannot help you with. In such cases you need the help of a professional editor or an expert colleague.

4.13 In what areas might Grammarly, QuillBot, and Reverso be useful for assessing my text?

One major advantage of Grammarly and QuillBot over ChatGPT is that they highlight the changes they have made, and give you explanations as to why they think you made a mistake with your English. ChatGPT does not do this automatically. This is slightly counterbalanced by the fact that often ChatGPT corrects mistakes that the other two applications have not noticed.

If you paste a text into Grammarly, it will tell you:

- what words or phrases it thinks are grammatical incorrect
- make suggestions for punctuation
- tell you how clear and engaging your text is
- assess the level of formality
- identify possible spelling mistakes
- suggest ways to reduce the length of certain phrases (premium version only)
- alert you to possible plagiarism (premium version only) – but beware such AI detectors have been found to have a bias against non-native speakers

Other applications such as QuillBot and Reverso have similar functions. They provide:

- explanations for the mistakes you have made so that you can improve your writing skills
- improve the flow of your text
- rewrite overly complex sentences

Again, the advantages of these applications over ChatGPT is that they visualize all the modifications that they are suggesting, whereas ChatGPT simply makes the changes without highlighting what it has done. The disadvantages is that many of the features require you to pay for the premium versions.

Of course, the main advantage of ChatGPT compared to the applications mentioned above is that you can ask it questions and prompt to follow specific tasks. This is why in this book I have focused on ChatGPT rather than other AI tools that can be used for editing. At the time of writing this book, Curie was not available but is definitely worth checking out if you want to edit an entire paper with a single click of your mouse.

For more suggestions on using these other applications see Chapter 11 of *English for Academic Research: Grammar, Usage and Style* (2023 edn.).

4.14 How can I convert a text in my own language into an accurate text in English? How can I combine my use of Google Translate and ChatGPT?

It is possible to produce a 99% accurate text in terms of English grammar and vocabulary by starting with a text written in your own language and the using a combination of Google Translate and ChatGPT. This works particularly well if your language is one of the world's major languages.

> Of course, I am only talking about accuracy in English. The procedure outlined below will NOT automatically produce a good quality text in terms of content, style, and readability (see 1.4). The quality of the version in your language has to be high in order for it to be high in English.

Below (T1) is a text written in Chinese by one of my PhD students, Yiyuan Han, who is studying at a university in the UK.

T1 在我的个人体验中，中国和英国大学生活的最大差异集中在宿舍生活上:在中国时，我和另外三名女同学共享一间价格低廉的寝室及其所附带的浴室；而在英国就读期间，我个人则体验了虽然价位不一但却与在中国大相径庭的居住模式:无论价格几何，至少都有着独立卧室与更多私人空间。我很怀念和我本科期间室友间的深厚友谊，但我们也一致同意如果有更多私人空间的话生活会更加舒适，尽管在中国密集的人口和较低的大学费用下这可能并不太可行。

This is how GT translated it.

T2 In my personal experience, the biggest difference between university life in China and the UK is in dormitory life: in China, I shared a cheap dormitory and its attached bathroom with three other female classmates; while studying in the UK During this period, I personally experienced a living pattern that was quite different from that in China although the price was different: no matter what the price was, at least there was a separate bedroom and more private space. I miss the deep friendship I had with my roommate during my undergraduate years, but we also agreed that life would be more comfortable with more personal space, although that might not be feasible given China's dense population and lower college costs.

The translation is reasonably accurate, but at times does not sound like a native speaker. This is also because Yiyuan's punctuation is different from that used in English.

So how could you get a better translation?

Well one solution, which I discuss in Chapter 3, is to work on the original Chinese version. Yiyuan's version only contains two periods (.) in a paragraph which in English is over 100 words long. Long sentences are more difficult for AI to interpret than short ones. So I used this prompt with ChatGPT:

Please use shorter sentences in the following Chinese text.

This produced this shorter text, which now contains three rather than two sentences.

T3 在中国，我和三名女同学住在一个便宜的寝室，有共用浴室。在英国，我有独立卧室和更多私人空间，虽然价位不同。我怀念本科时的室友友谊，但我们都同意更多私人空间会更舒适。在中国的高人口和低费用下，这可能不太可行。

I then used GT to translate the above text (T3), which produced T4 below.

T4 In China, I lived with three female classmates in a cheap dorm room with a shared bathroom. In the UK, I had a separate bedroom and more private space, albeit at a different price point. I miss the friendship of my roommates from undergrad, but we all agreed that more private space would be more comfortable. With China's high population and low costs, this may not be as feasible.

I then submitted T4 with the following prompt:

Correct any English language mistakes in the following text.

This produced T5.

T5 While in China, I lived with three female classmates in an inexpensive dorm room with a shared bathroom. In the UK, I had a separate bedroom and more private space, albeit at a different price point. Although I miss the companionship of my undergraduate roommates, we all agreed that having more personal space would be more comfortable. Unfortunately, this may not be as feasible in China due to its high population and low costs.

Yiyuan speaks good English but I don't think she could have ever produced such an accurate version as T5. The only rather strange phrase is *albeit at a different price point*, but the meaning is clear.

However, what is not clear, and which was not clear in the original Chinese, is what she means by 'low costs'. This highlights how important it is for the text in your own language to be totally clear.

In summary, the steps I followed are:

1. Write the text in your own language.
2. Analyse your text and simplify it as much as possible. Cut as much as you can, and divide up any long sentences. This is called 'pre-editing'.
3. Submit this text to machine translation into English.
4. Submit the output to ChatGPT with the prompt: Correct any English language mistakes.

The benefits:

- You have much more control of the final output if you work hard on the version you write in your own language.
- You will produce a more accurate version in English than if you wrote in English from scratch, or than if you submitted the text in your own language without any pre-editing.

Note that in reality you wouldn't be

- submitting such a short text. Clearly the longer the text, the greater the chances of AI getting something wrong
- able to judge the exact quality of the final English output yourself
- sure that your paper would be accepted for publication, because the process I have suggested doesn't account for the fact that the overall structure, logical sequence and general readability of what you have written may be poor even though the English is perfect

You might also object by saying Yiyuan's text is non-technical. I chose it precisely because it is non-technical so that all readers, whatever their area of study, could understand it. However, my experiments with technical texts have given the same results.

Chapter 5
How to interact with a chatbot and simulate typical scenarios that take place in academia

5.1 Introduction

This chapter shows you how to set up 'conversations' with a bot in order to:

- increase the chances that the bot does what you want it to do;
- get the bot to tell you how to improve a prompt that you have just inserted – this is known as metaprompting
- role playing particular situations in your academic life (such as going for a job interview, socializing at a conference)
- get the right tone and style in the texts that a bot generates for you

5.2 Avoid ambiguous and vague language in your prompts

To ensure that your conversation with the bot is effective:

- Provide a clear context: Who are you? What field are you working in? What are your individual circumstances?
- State your desired outcome: Clearly express what you expect from the response. This helps set the context and enables the model to understand the goal of the prompt.
- Use simple language: The bot has a large vocabulary and can understand complex language. However, if you use clear and simple language it will make it easier for the bot to understand your prompt and provide a response that is easy for you to understand.

A. Wallwork, *AI-Assisted Writing and Presenting in English*, English for Academic Research, https://doi.org/10.1007/978-3-031-48147-5_5

- Avoid jargon: If your prompt includes technical or industry-specific jargon, it's important to define those terms so that the bot understands what you're asking.
- Be careful of using words in your prompt that are very subjective. For example, what do these adjectives really mean: *appropriate, effective, smart, successful*?
- Don't refer to very broad concepts such as *science, writing, technology, success, gender, politics, globalization*. You make think that specifications such as the following are more specific, but in reality they are still too generic: *the effects of climate change, recent technological advances, historical events that shaped the modern world, the relationship between nature and human behavior*. The bot needs to know which kinds of *effect*, which *technologies*, which type of *events* and where they took place, etc.

5.3 Meta-prompting: getting the bot to tell you how to improve your prompt

I submitted the following **PROMPT**:

> **Summarize the key concepts of the internet of things.**

The bot then gave me a 445 word response made up of an introduction, 13 bullet points, and a conclusion. It was comprehensive, but didn't really focus on the areas I was interested in. I then wrote:

> **Thank you. Please could you tell me how I could have improved the prompt that I gave you?**

The bot suggested this expanded version of my **PROMPT**:

> **Can you provide me with a comprehensive overview of the fundamental concepts that define the Internet of Things (IoT)? I'm interested in understanding how interconnected devices, data collection through sensors, data transmission methods, cloud computing's role, data analytics, security concerns, and the potential impact on various industries all come together in the realm of IoT.**

The bot's version of my prompt is clearly a lot better than my original. I strongly suggest that you get the bot's help with rewriting your prompts:

- You can immediately input the bot's suggested prompt and see its new response, which should be more suitable than the one produced with your original prompt.
- You can base future prompts on what you now know the bot thinks will generate the best response for your needs.

At the beginning of a new chat, you can tell the bot that whenever you insert a new **PROMPT**, it should first respond by rewriting your prompt. If you are then happy with this new **PROMPT**, you can instruct the bot to use it:

> **You have provided me with a better prompt than my original. Please could your answer your prompt.**

5.4 Consider using the bot in your own language too

It might be worth you using the chatbot in your own language: (i) if you are writing the whole text of your paper in your native language, then you could use the bot as a kind of content editor to review each section (or key paragraphs within a section – see 4.10); (ii) even if you are writing from scratch in English, having the bot's input in your own language might be easier for you to understand. Alternatively, you can translate the bot's English output into your own language to make sure you have understood the advice correctly.

Chatting with your bot in two languages may give you more interesting results than simply using English and getting the bot to 'regenerate' its response.

The more you work on the text in your own language (i.e. a language over which you have total control), the better the final result will be.

5.5 Effective chats and role plays

When you want to conduct a chat with a bot, i.e. not just to ask a single question or give a single task, you can craft your initial **PROMPT** so that the bot will use that **PROMPT** in all subsequent responses that it gives you.

One way to do this is to give the bot a role. And you can specify how the bot should carry out that role. Below are examples of **PROMPTS** to set up two different role plays.

> **Imagine you are my teacher, explain one step at a time so that I have the opportunity to ask you for a clarification if I need to.**

> **Please act as a devil's advocate and weigh up the pros and cons of becoming a vegan. Give me one response at a time, so that I can react to it and ask further questions.**

Your **PROMPT** could be short without too many details:

> **Play the role of an English language editor. I will submit to you a series of texts written in my poor English!**

Or it could be much more detailed.

> **Play the role of a research proposal writer. I will provide you with a broad research topic, and your task will be to compose a proposal outlining the specific focus of the research, the research questions to be addressed, and the methods to be employed for conducting the research. The proposal should also include a literature review summarizing existing research on the topic and showcasing the significance and relevance of the proposed study.**

Note how in the above **PROMPT**, the interactor/user provides the bot with various texts that will enable the bot to generate relevant questions.

Here are some general guidelines of how to engage in an effective chat or role playing scenario.

1. BE CLEAR AND SPECIFIC: Clearly state your question or request to help the bot understand your intention accurately.
2. ASK FOR CLARIFICATION: If you receive a response that is unclear or not what you expected, ask for clarification.

3. NARROW DOWN OPTIONS: If the bot provides too many options or you want more specific answers, you can ask it to choose the best option from a list or compare two specific choices.

4. SEEK EXPLANATIONS: If the bot provides a result or answer, but you're interested in understanding the reasoning behind it, ask for an explanation.

5. ENGAGE IN A CONVERSATION: The bot can conversations, so ask follow-up questions, build on previous answers, or respond to its statements.

6. EXPERIMENT AND ITERATE: Experiment with different phrasings, approaches, or requests. The bot can sometimes provide more insightful responses with slight variations in your questions or prompts.

The aim is to create a back-and-forth dialogue to ensure a more interactive experience. This involves asking follow-up questions, helping the bot to refine its answers, asking for clarifications, re-specifying what you want if the bot goes off track, and staying engaged with bot by feedback on the bot's performance (i.e. is it doing what you hoped it would?).

When you have finished your chat and you want the bot to do some completely unconnected task, then press 'new chat', 'new topic'. This action provides the bot with a fresh start, preventing any confusion or merging of unrelated subjects.

5.6 Role playing with the bot: (1) interview process

Here is another example where it would be useful to provide additional texts (underlined for the purposes of this example in the prompt below) in order to help the bot play its role effectively.

Play the role of an interviewer. I will be the candidate, and you will ask me interview questions for the position I'm applying for. Your role is solely to respond as the interviewer. Please refrain from providing the entire conversation at once. Conduct the interview by asking questions one by one, just like an interviewer would, and wait for my answers. I am applying for a job as junior biotechnologist. I will submit to you in sequence my CV, my application letter, and the job post I am responding to.

I submitted the above **PROMPT**, but without the accompanying documentation. I kept my answers short as I was mainly interested in the questions it would generate. It produced the following:

Interviewer: Good day! Thank you for joining us today. Let's begin with some questions to get to know you better.

1. Could you please introduce yourself and tell us about your background in biotechnology?

I first became interested in biotechnology in 10th grade at school. Blah blah blah

Interviewer: That's great to hear! It's always fascinating to see early interests develop into career aspirations. Now, let's delve into your educational background.

1. What is your academic background in biotechnology? Could you tell us about your relevant degrees, courses, or any specialized training you have undertaken?

I have a degree in x, a Master's in y, and now I am in my final year as a PhD student studying z.

Interviewer: Impressive academic journey! It's evident that you have dedicated significant time and effort to your education in the field of biotechnology. Now, let's shift our focus to practical experience.

1. Can you please share any relevant work or research experience you have gained in the field of biotechnology? This could include internships, projects, or collaborations.

I have done x, y and z. I think these three experiences have given me very different insights into the world of biotechnology.

Interviewer: That's wonderful to hear that you have gained diverse experiences in biotechnology. It's important to have a well-rounded understanding of the field. Now, let's discuss your specific skills and abilities.

1. What technical skills do you possess that are relevant to the field of biotechnology? This could include laboratory techniques, data analysis, programming languages, or any other specialized skills.

I found the responses rather tedious as they all began with a comment on my previous question and basically all followed the same style. However, they do give you an idea of the kind of comments an interviewer may make.

But if you are not happy with the way the bot plays its role, then you need to tweak the **PROMPT**.

> **Sorry, but essentially I am just interested in the questions. I don't need you to comment on my answers. However, please keep the link phrases, e.g. Now, let's shift our focus to ... Please also vary the style of your questions. Occasionally ask a difficult question.**

The bot then proceeded to ask more challenging questions, but still complimented me on my answers! The questions were all about my technical skills. So I then wanted the bot to focus on me and my personality. This is what the bot produced:

Certainly! Let's shift the focus to your personality and personal qualities.

1. In your opinion, what are your strongest attributes or qualities that make you well-suited for a career in biotechnology? How do these qualities contribute to your professional success?
2. Biotechnology often requires attention to detail and meticulousness. Can you describe how you ensure accuracy and precision in your work? How do you handle situations that demand a high level of detail-oriented tasks?
3. Problem-solving and critical thinking skills are vital in the field of biotechnology. Can you provide an example of a time when you applied these skills to overcome a scientific or technical challenge? How did you analyze the problem and arrive at a solution?
4. Effective communication is essential in scientific research and collaboration. Describe your communication style and how you ensure clear and concise communication with colleagues, supervisors, and team members.
5. As a junior biotechnologist, continuous learning and professional development are crucial. How do you stay motivated and engaged in your field? Can you share any instances where you took the initiative to expand your knowledge or skills beyond your academic or work requirements?

Feel free to share your thoughts and experiences related to these questions.

As you can see, the bot did not do as I asked it in the initial prompt (*Conduct the interview by asking questions one by one)* and instead was asking multiple questions. So again, you would need to tweak the bot to remind it of its role.

I finished my chat by asking for advice on how to answer an unethical question. Here is the response:

> Ask me a question that would be illegal for an interviewer to ask. Then write me an answer to the question which highlights politely that I am not legally obliged to answer that question.

> As an AI language model, I am programmed to follow ethical guidelines and promote fair and respectful communication. It is important to note that I cannot generate or endorse illegal content, including questions that an interviewer would be prohibited from asking.
>
> However, I can provide you with a response that politely addresses the situation where a question may not be legally appropriate:
>
> Interviewer: "What is your religious affiliation?"
>
> Candidate: "Thank you for considering me for this opportunity. While I appreciate your interest, it is important to note that questions related to religious affiliation are not relevant to my qualifications for this position. I believe that my skills, experience, and professional achievements are the key factors that should be considered in assessing my suitability for the role."
>
> Remember, during an actual interview, if you encounter an illegal or inappropriate question, you have the right to politely redirect or decline to answer while maintaining your professionalism.

The bot's response highlights a number of points:

- The bot has an ethical stance, or claims to have one. This means that it may not help with any situation that it considers to be unethical.
- The bot's summary paragraph is useful advice.
- The bot's answer for the candidate is unnecessarily long. You are unlikely to be able to remember the exact wording, and such a 'technical' answer is likely to take the interviewer by surprise. Essentially, you need to be critical of a bot's responses, particularly when they regard a delicate situation. A simpler (and easier to remember) answer would be: "I am afraid I can't answer that question". Or: "Sorry but I don't think I am legally obliged to answer that question".

In any case, using a role-playing exercise is a great way to simulate an interview, which then enables you to prepare your responses in advance. However, don't expect a real interviewer to be so friendly and accommodating!

5.7 Role playing with the bot: (2) socializing at a conference

A key part of academic life is attending a conference and participating the social events. A bot can help you practise for conversations at a social dinner. Here is a **PROMPT** that you could adapt.

> **I am a young PhD student. I come from Albania. I am going to an international conference where I will meet other people in my field. I am worried about having social interactions, particularly at dinners. Initially, I would like you to take the role of the person sitting opposite me at the dinner table. You are 60 years old and are an expert in my field. I want to role play a conversation with you, where we initially talk about work but then quickly move on to non-work aspects. Please begin with a question that I can ask you, then answer it yourself, and then ask me a question. Is this clear?**

The bot replied as follows.

Of course, that sounds clear. I'll start by taking on the role of the 60-year-old expert in your field sitting across from you at the dinner table.

You: Good evening. It's a pleasure to meet you. I'm curious to know what initially sparked your interest in our field.

Expert: Good evening! It's a pleasure to meet you too. Well, my interest in our field actually began during my undergraduate years. I had an exceptional professor who ignited my passion for this subject with their enthusiasm and innovative research. That experience set me on this path.

Now, I'd like to learn more about your journey. How did you first become interested in our field, and what inspired you to pursue a PhD?

If you think the tone is too formal, then you can tweak your prompt:

Sorry, could you use less formal language.

Of course, I can be less formal. Let's try that again.

You: Hey there! Nice to meet you. I'm curious, what got you interested in our field in the first place?

Expert: Hey! Great to meet you too. You know, I got into this field during my undergrad days. I had this amazing professor who got me all excited about it. Their passion and cool research projects just hooked me.

Now, I'm curious about you. What led you to our field, and what made you decide to pursue a PhD?

The bot's response above is actually rather too informal now, so you would need to tweak the **PROMPT** again:

Sorry, now it's a bit too informal. Please try something more neutral.

Later in the conversation, you can ask the bot to do other tasks.

OK, can you now list ten questions I could ask the expert that are not work-related and are not likely to cause embarrassment.

What kind of questions should I not ask?

In answer to the second **PROMPT** the bot responded as below. To me they all seem sensible answers and include some that I myself might not have thought to mention to my students, but which I think are extremely valid e.g. gossip or rumors (8).

To ensure a pleasant and respectful conversation at the dinner table, it's a good idea to avoid certain types of questions that could potentially be sensitive or uncomfortable. Here are some types of questions to avoid:

1. **Personal Finances:** Avoid asking about salary, income, or financial status. Money can be a sensitive topic for many people.
2. **Relationship Status:** Don't pry into someone's personal life by asking about their relationship status, romantic history, or family planning.
3. **Age-Related Questions:** Avoid questions about someone's age, especially if you suspect they might be sensitive about it.
4. **Health and Medical History:** Questions about health, medical conditions, or disabilities should generally be avoided, as they can be very personal and private.
5. **Controversial or Divisive Topics:** Stay away from discussing topics like politics, religion, or any other subjects that can lead to heated debates or disagreements.
6. **Negative or Critical Questions:** Avoid questions that could be interpreted as critical or judgmental, such as asking about someone's failures or regrets.
7. **Intrusive Personal Questions:** Questions about personal matters like someone's weight, physical appearance, or past mistakes should be off-limits.
8. **Gossip or Rumors:** Don't bring up gossip or rumors about the person or others in the field.
9. **Invasive or Overly Personal Questions:** Avoid asking overly personal questions that invade someone's privacy, such as their address, personal history, or deep-seated fears.
10. **Assumptions or Stereotypes:** Avoid making assumptions or stereotypical comments based on someone's background, nationality, or other characteristics.

Here are some other things you could ask the bot in relation to the role play about socializing at a conference.

> **As I said, I am Albanian. List some specific questions that I might be asked.**

The above **PROMPT** is very useful as it enables you to prepare in advance answers to such questions. By having ready well-formulated answers you are likely to impress your interlocutors and this could possibly lead to collaborations. Here are the questions that the bot produced. Clearly, you would need to decide which questions are likely to be asked, and how you would reply.

Certainly, when attending an international conference, you may encounter questions related to your background and culture as an Albanian. Here are some specific questions you might be asked:

1. "I've heard Albania has beautiful landscapes. Have you traveled around your country? Any must-visit places?"
2. "Albanian cuisine is known for its unique flavors. What's your favorite Albanian dish, and can you recommend a good place to try it?"
3. "I'm curious about the language. Can you teach me a basic Albanian phrase or tell me an interesting fact about the Albanian language?"
4. "Albania has a rich history. Are there any historical sites or museums in Albania that you would recommend visiting?"
5. "How would you describe the cultural traditions and customs in Albania? Is there a specific holiday or festival that you particularly enjoy celebrating?"
6. "I've heard about Albanian hospitality. Can you share a story or experience that reflects this aspect of your culture?"
7. "What's the music scene like in Albania? Are there any traditional Albanian musical instruments or genres you can tell us about?"
8. "Albania's recent history includes a transition from communism to democracy. How do you think this has influenced your generation and your academic pursuits?"
9. "I'm interested in learning more about Albanian art. Are there any famous Albanian artists or art movements that have made an impact on your country's culture?"
10. "Albania is known for its stunning coastlines. Have you had the chance to explore the beaches and coastal areas? Any recommendations for beach destinations?"

However, you need to be cautious about asking someone of another nationality such questions in the same format as the bot. The bots questions nearly all follow the same structure:

1. An affirmation about Albania.
2. A question in two parts separated by *or*. Alternatively, two different questions.

When asking questions at a social dinner, you need to vary the type of questions you ask otherwise it seems more like an interrogation!

Finally, here is a prompt about food, which is a very common subject of conversation at conferences.

In Albania our national dish is tavë kosi. Imagine I have to explain what it consists of and why it is so delicious. Please generate a series of simple sentences to do this. Remember, my level of English is not very advanced.

The above prompt produced:

Certainly, I'll help you explain Tavë Kosi in simple sentences:

1. Tavë Kosi is a special dish from Albania.
2. It's made with tender lamb meat, rice, and yogurt.
3. The lamb is cooked until it's very soft and flavorful.
4. Then, it's mixed with rice and a creamy yogurt sauce.
5. The yogurt makes it taste really smooth and rich.
6. Tavë Kosi has a unique taste because of the combination of flavors.
7. The yogurt gives it a slightly tangy and creamy flavor.
8. The lamb adds a delicious, savory taste to the dish.
9. It's often baked in the oven until it gets a golden crust on top.
10. People in Albania love it because it's both comforting and tasty.

Asking the bot to write in simple English will really help you as you will be more able to remember the phrases and use them with confidence at the conference.

5.8 Role playing with the bot: (3) pronunciation tutor

You can also get a bot to help you with your pronunciation. Here is an example:

> **I am Iranian. Act as if you are a pronunciation guide for Farsi speakers of English. I will provide you with a list of words that I find difficult to pronounce. Respond with their pronunciations, without any translations. However, I want you to take into account that I am Iranian. So please point out any typical problems that an Iranian might have with these English words. Here are the first three words: business, candidate, definitely.**

Below is the response:

Sure, I'd be happy to help! Here are the pronunciations for the five words you provided, along with some tips and notes for an Iranian speaker:

1. Business: /ˈbɪznəs/ (BIZ-nuhs)

- Note that the "s" at the end of the word is pronounced as a "z" sound. Also, the stress is on the first syllable.

2. Candidate: /ˈkændɪdət/ (KAN-dih-duht)

- The stress is on the first syllable, and the "d" and "t" sounds at the end of the word can be difficult for some Iranian speakers to differentiate. The "a" sound in the first syllable is pronounced like the "a" in "man."

3. Definitely: /ˈdɛfənɪtli/ (DEF-uh-nit-lee)

- The stress is on the second syllable. The "i" sound in the second syllable is pronounced like the "ee" in "tree." Iranian speakers may have difficulty with the "d" and "t" sounds in this word as well.

The advantage of this role-playing approach is that you set up an entire conversation, without you constantly having to write the same or similar prompts. However, bots are not always predictable and may randomly start ignoring your initial prompts. So each time you insert a new text, check that the bot is still following your prompt.

For more on using AI to help with your pronunciation see 7.8.

Note that on occasions that require value judgements or entail ethical considerations, the bot may not agree to provide you with an answer to your question. And although a bot is not human, it pays to treat it with respect. In the words of a bot:

When writing your prompt, it's important to be respectful and avoid language that is offensive or discriminatory. I am programmed to respond in a respectful and helpful manner, and I expect the same in return.

Chapter 6
Communicating with lay audiences

6.1 Introduction: Why do you need to communicate with a lay audience?

There are various occasions when you need to tell a lay (i.e. non-expert) audience about your research, for example:

- a plain language summary (often required by journals, it is like a non-technical abstract)
- an oral presentation at a multi-disciplinary conference, seminar, webinar etc
- a project proposal: there is often a section specifically for non-experts outlining the benefits for society in general of conducting the research you are proposing
- a teacher training session
- your institution's website
- blog posts or other social media
- informal emails
- a post on Academia, LinkedIn, ResearchGate etc

Such occasions allow you to communicate your work to non-specialists, policymakers, journalists, or interested individuals who may benefit from understanding the research findings without getting lost in technical jargon or intricate details.

Writing for a lay audience is important. But you have to believe in why you are doing it.

A. Wallwork, *AI-Assisted Writing and Presenting in English*, English for Academic Research, https://doi.org/10.1007/978-3-031-48147-5_6

"For researchers to commit the time and effort to learn the skills and write good summaries, they need to believe that public engagement is one possible approach to improving the quality, relevance and impact of their work." https://www.dcc.ac.uk/guidance/how-guides/write-lay-summary

Your aim is to communicate both to the scientific community and the general public in a way that is:

- accessible: people need to be able to find your work, understand the content introduced, and have no difficulty with the language used to describe this content
- informative: your audience need to be able to exploit the knowledge they have found in your work
- credible and transparent: funders need to be encouraged to finance your work

This chapter shows you how to use ChatGPT (and similar tools) to write for a lay audience. It also highlights the limitations of these tools in being able to tell you that your text is suitable for a lay audience.

Using a bot to help you write a presentation or email, is dealt with in Chapter 7 and Chapter 8, respectively.

6.2 Style, tone and voice

When crafting a **PROMPT**, tell the bot what style you want and what the level of understanding is of the readers of the text that you will produce from the bot's response. You need to do this when

i) generating a text from scratch:

> **Write a short introduction of 150 words or less for a presentation for a lay audience. The topic is testing shampoos on animals. Use a non-technical style. Use short sentences. Do not assume that the audience have any prior knowledge of this topic.**
>
> **Create four threads/tweets in a typical social media tone that convey xyz.**
>
> **Look at this About section for my academic blog. Create a LinkedIn post introducing my blog to a wider audience using an engaging and friendly tone, but still professional.**
>
> **Explain xyz to me imagining that I am 11 years old.**

ii) asking the bot to correct your English:

I am an academic. Correct the English of this email to a colleague. Use a neutral style. The colleague is the same age as me but is not a friend, we have never met.

iii) rewriting an existing text for a new audience:

Rewrite this text on using animals for testing cosmetics. Make it suitable for a group of high-school children in a town where there are several laboratories that use animals for testing.

This text is a post on Academia. I want to post it on XYZ. Please rewrite it to make it sound more engaging. I want to encourage readers to click on the link to my paper.

iv) writing a text in a similar style to a text written by another author. One way to do this is to get the bot to identify what style the other author has used:

What kind of tone is the following text written in? Give me specific examples of sentences that highlight the tone you have identified.

The bot will respond with something like the text below and also give a series of example sentences that confirm that the bot has identified the right tone.

The tone of the given text can be described as informative and formal. It provides factual information about xxx, its history, and its unique position within the university system. The language used is professional and objective, focusing on presenting details about the institution.

If you are sure that the bot has correctly identified the style of the other author, you can then submit your own text using the following **PROMPT**:

Using the informative and formal tone that you have just identified, please rewrite the following text.

When doing this, ensure that consecutive **PROMPT**s are part of the same chat with the bot. Do not start a new chat.

6.3 Skills needed for writing texts that will be read by non-experts

Writing a text for a non-academic audience entails facilitating the reader's understanding of your text by:

- distinguishing between what is and is not important – first in your own mind before you start writing, and then for the reader
- not automatically assuming that reader will or will not know something
- not automatically assuming that reader will understand why you have told them something
- explaining everything through clear concrete examples
- prioritizing examples over theory, and ensuring that if it is essential to mention any theory then this theory should be introduced through an example – so i) example, ii) theory
- making it very clear to readers how one idea builds on another
- deleting redundant words and expressions: *in the last few decades, it is worth noting that, in particular*
- avoiding the continuous use of words such as *additionally, in addition, also, furthermore* – these words tend to indicate that you are piling up ideas with no logical order and using these words to show an apparent logical connection where there is in fact no such connection
- not leaving the reader wondering why you have mentioned something
- remembering that simple language does not detract but instead helps to highlight your message
- not trying to demonstrate that you are smarter than the reader

In reality, all the points mentioned above are true for writing for an academic audience, not only for a lay audience. They are simply good guidelines for writing clearly.

6.4 Your use of the English language is probably not the main problem. Instead, assume that the content needs improving

If you want a bot to radically improve the content of your text, it helps if you assume that your text is not good. You then you need to coax the bot to take a negative view of your text and to look at it with a very critical eye. You can do this whether your text is in your own language (ChatGPT can deal with most languages) or in English.

I suggest that you begin by writing a page or two: not the whole document because the advice you get from the bot you can then apply directly when you are writing additional text.

So submit your two pages with the following prompt:

> **How clear is the following text for a lay audience?**

The bot will tell you something like 'the text is moderately clear for a lay audience, but some parts may require further explanation or simplification'.

Get the bot to suggest a revised version that is more accessible. Then analyze the revised version that the bot has generated. Ask yourself these questions:

1. Does the bot's version use a similar number of words to my text, but with more paragraphs?
2. Is the average sentence length shorter than in my version?
3. Are concepts explained more clearly?
4. Do any very modified sentences indicate perhaps that my original sentence was contorted and unclear?

Another approach is to use **PROMPT**s where the bot takes on a specific role. For example you instruct the bot to 'act as if you were a university student' or 'an audience listening to this speech'. Below are some example **PROMPT**s.

> **Write a list of questions that students might ask their teacher when they have read the text to understand it more in detail.**

> **If the text were used as an introduction to a presentation, what questions might the audience be asking themselves as they listen?**

Imagine you are a university student. The lecturer has begun their presentation with the following words. What questions might you be asking in your head as you listen to their presentation?

This time imagine you are 16. What might you be thinking as you listen?

Your aim is to find out how your readers and audience might interpret your text. You can get the bot to take a very critical stance by informing it that you already know that your text is not good, but that you are not entirely sure why it is not good.

My teacher has told me that the following is not a good introduction to an oral presentation. Why?

The bot will generate a list of areas where improvements could be made. So in your next **PROMPT** get the bot to provide suggestions on how to implement the improvements that it has outlined.

If you get the bot involved in your writing process right from the start, this will help you as you continue drafting your text.

6.5 How to critically analyse what you have written

Use the questions below to analyse your text (or sentences and paragraphs within the text).

1. Will the audience / reader be clear about what I am trying to do and why I decided to do it?
2. Am I making assumptions about what they will and will not know?
3. Will the connections between one sentence/paragraph be logical for the reader?
4. I have used some specific technical words. I know why I have used them and I know what they mean. Will the readers know?
5. Do I need more examples and less theory?
6. Can I replace any abstract words with a concrete equivalent?
7. I am particularly pleased with this sentence. In reality could I delete it? In fact, could I cut what I have written by 25 percent without eliminating any useful content?
8. It's taken me hours to produce this and it sounds really good. But will it actually add any value for the audience? Does it actually mean anything?

When writing a text for any kind of audience – expert or lay – keep everything as simple as possible (see Chapter 4 of *English for Writing Research Papers*, 2023 edn. to learn some rules for concise clear writing).

- Do not try to be clever.
- Do not make the audience feel stupid.
- Do not force the audience to make connections. Instead, make the connections for your audience.
- Do not use ten words when one is sufficient.

You can still be creative, and you can still express complex concepts, but you have to enable the audience to follow you each step of the way.

6.6 The bot doesn't always get it right

> The suggestions given in this chapter are NOT foolproof. Sometimes the bot gets it wrong. The problem is that you may not be aware that it is wrong. So if you are producing a text that is really important, then you need to show it to a native speaker.

This section covers two common issues:

- your ability or inability to assess whether a bot's 'expert' advice is good or not
- what to do when your initial prompt fails to have the desired effect

For the purposes of showing you how the bot can seem like an expert but doesn't necessarily give you good advice, I drafted a speech to be given as an introduction to a teacher training session. Such sessions are generally quite informal and are designed to be engaging and interactive. To test the bot's lack of utility, I wrote the speech in a ridiculously formal way beginning with: *Ladies and gentlemen, esteemed educators, and fellow language enthusiasts ...*

I then submitted my speech to the bot with the following **PROMPT**:

> **Below is an introduction to some sessions I will be doing for trainee teachers. I think it might be a little formal. What do you think? How could I make it more friendly?**

The bot then proceeded to rewrite it, rather than comment on it. This is a typical misunderstanding. So I gave it another prompt:

> **Sorry, I didn't want you to rewrite it. I just want the answer to this question. Is it too formal? If it is suggest ways I could make the text more fun for the trainee teachers?**

The bot then told me that yes, it was too formal, and produced the following advice:

1. Use inclusive and casual language: Instead of "Ladies and gentlemen, esteemed educators, and fellow language enthusiasts," you could start with a more inclusive and friendly greeting like "Hello everyone," or "Hey there, fellow educators and language enthusiasts!"
2. Set a relaxed tone: Begin with a warm and welcoming statement, such as "I'm thrilled to have you all here today," or "I hope you're ready for an exciting and enjoyable training session!"
3. Inject enthusiasm and excitement: Show your passion for the topic by using energetic language. For example, you could say, "Get ready to embark on an absolutely thrilling training session!" or "Prepare yourselves for a journey into the enchanting world of language acquisition!"
4. Ask engaging questions: Instead of posing the question in a formal manner, make it more conversational and interactive. For instance, you could ask, "Imagine learning a language just for the sheer joy of it. Which language would you choose and why? Let's hear your fascinating answers!"
5. Use relatable examples and anecdotes: Share personal stories, interesting anecdotes, or relatable experiences related to language learning. This can help create a friendly and relatable atmosphere.
6. Incorporate humor: Sprinkle in some light-hearted humor to keep the session lively. For instance, you could say, "We're about to dive into the wild and wonderful world of language learning. Get ready for a rollercoaster ride filled with linguistic twists and turns!"
7. Encourage interactive activities: Include interactive activities, group discussions, or small breakout sessions to foster engagement and create a more enjoyable learning environment.

So what's the problem?

The advice given at the beginning of each bullet is excellent. However, the example sentences, particularly in points 1, 3 and 5 are not appropriate. They are too enthusiastic and contain too many adjectives. With most Anglo audiences, you would lose all credibility almost immediately if you talk in this overly effusive way.

It is not straightforward for a non-native English speaker to understand whether a bot's advice is good or not. If you have any doubts, and the text you are writing is for an important audience, then you should enlist the help of a qualified native speaker. You don't need to send them your entire text, just a short extract would be enough for them to tell you whether the tone and level of formality are appropriate or not.

Another issue is that the bot might not follow your prompt first time (or second, or third!). Below is a series of prompts that highlight how to re-prompt when the bot does not initially complete the task in the way you wanted.

> **The following text is from the homepage of an academic institute's website. What information do you think could be removed?**
>
> **Sorry, I didn't ask you to correct it. I wanted to know what information could be removed in order to make it more concise.**
>
> **Sorry, again. I want to know which information has been removed. I do not want to see a more concise version.**
>
> **Great. Thank you. Generally speaking, what kind of information should be highlighted on a university's homepage?**

6.7 A note on gender pronouns

When writing for or talking to a lay audience, you will often be using personal pronouns. A bot may or may not identify potential misusages regarding gender and inclusivity. So it is best to bear in mind the following:

Refrain from using masculine pronouns to represent generic individuals (e.g., "the user .. he .."). Instead, where possible, use plural forms (e.g., "users ... they") for gender-neutral references.

In academic and scientific writing, the use of gender-neutral language is generally preferred to ensure inclusivity and avoid potential biases. Instead of using "he" or "she" to refer to an individual, use gender-neutral alternatives. Here are some options:

- SINGULAR "THEY": This is a widely accepted and increasingly common gender-neutral pronoun. For example, instead of "he/she conducted the experiment," you could write "they conducted the experiment."
- PLURAL FORMS AND PASSIVE VOICE: You can use plural forms to avoid gendered pronouns. For instance, instead of "he/she can use this method," you can write "researchers can use this method" or "this method can be used".
- TITLES AND ROLE: Instead of using pronouns, you can refer to individuals by their titles, roles, or descriptors.

For more on this issue see Chapter 10 *Personal pronouns, names, titles* in the companion volume to this series: *English for Academic Research: Grammar, Usage and Style* (2023 edn.).

6.8 Understanding what a lay audience wants: examples, anecdotes, statistics

I used to run a collaborative blog where we invited teachers to share their experiences in the classroom and to recount any difficulties or amusing / insightful episodes that they had had in settling in the country where they teach.

Often in blogs people write in a very abstract way. On the other hand, the best posts tend to give a sense of the writer's personality and recount specific things that have happened to them.
Here is an example from a teacher working in a US state that borders with Mexico:

> *Many of the students I encounter are coming from experiences vastly different from my own upbringing so I find I can learn as much from the students as I can possibly teach them. I am privileged to learn about new cultures, traditions, and have fun expressing my inner child through laughter, smiles, and silliness when appropriate.*

The above text appears to have a lot of concrete words: *upbringing, culture, tradition, inner child, laughter* etc. But such words are still abstract. The reader isn't actually told:

- what makes the teacher's experiences and upbringing different from their students
- what exactly the teacher learns from the students
- what kind of traditions
- what precisely they mean by 'silliness'

And what will the reader be able to remember after having read that teacher's text?

For YOU the words *upbringing, culture, tradition, inner child, laughter* mean something specific when you use them to recount something that has happened to you. But the READER doesn't share the same memories as you, so they can't picture what you have in your mind. For the reader, such words are just words, they don't trigger any emotion.

When you write for a lay audience (and, in my opinion, even an expert audience) you need to be much more explicit. I suggest you cover less ground (i.e. fewer points), but ensure that the points that you do make are supported with examples and stories and statistics. This will make your writing come alive. Here is a revised version:

> *At least 80% of my students have had a vastly different upbringing from my own. They have had to cross the border from Mexico to the US. One even told me that she had been hidden in the roof space of a car when entering the States. Their parents have had to struggle to find work, mostly cleaning jobs, and often double shifts, so that they rarely see their children. Many of my kids learned to read by themselves and taught their siblings. I have learned about courage, independence*

and persistence. I am also privileged to learn about new cultures and traditions. I was once invited to their Day of the Dead festival and ... ... There's a lot of laughter, particularly when I try to speak Spanish for them! It makes them see that their teacher can be vulnerable too.

The original version was 56 words, the new version 143. Consequently, giving examples means using more words, so that you have less time/space to say other things. This does not matter. You are never going to be asked to recount everything you know about a topic. Instead what you say is a kind of entry point into your readers' and audience's minds – you want to stimulate them so that they will want to know more from you.

By using examples and anecdotes, readers and audience will be able to visualize what you are recounting. They will be able to connect with both you and what you say. The result will be a much more pleasurable experience – not just for them, but for you too. And if it has been pleasurable, informative and useful, then people will want to know more, will want to contact you, will want to talk about your work with other people.

When you write a blog post, or any kind of text, you can enlist a bot's support through prompts such as:

> **The following text is from a blog post on xyz. What information do you think is missing?**
>
> **Suggest three ways I could make my post more reader friendly.**
>
> **Write an 00-character meta description for my post.**
>
> **Imagine you are reader of my post. What might you be thinking as you read?**
>
> **Generate 10 different comments a reader might leave on my post. Include some controversial ones, and/or ones that disagree with what I have written.**

In response to the last **PROMPT** listed above the bot will generate a variety of comments that are likely to include the following: support, disagreement, shared personal experience, controversial viewpoint, skeptical opinion, and cultural perspective. The controversial and skeptical ones are particularly useful as they may point out to you areas that you had not considered but which are worth you taking into account in your final draft of the post.

Chapter 7
Presentations

7.1 Introduction

Section 7.2 talks in general about the concept of simplicity, particularly in the way you write and deliver your presentation speech.

The other sections of this chapter highlight the benefits of using a chatbot to generate:

- a script for your slides
- the text of your slides
- possible questions your audience might ask you, plus the answers

Many of the sections relate to a presentation in the field of biorobotics, which is the study of how biological organisms (e.g. plants) can be used to develop new technologies. This chapter does not talk about doing presentations online. This is covered in Chapter 12 of *Giving an Academic Presentation in English* (Springer, 2021).

A. Wallwork, *AI-Assisted Writing and Presenting in English*, English for Academic Research, https://doi.org/10.1007/978-3-031-48147-5_7

7.2 Simplicity

How do you prefer to receive the information given in someone's presentation?

1. In a way which tests your concentration and brain because you have to work out the meaning yourself?
2. In a simple format, covering everything that you need to know, with minimal mental effort yet still simulating?

In Anglo societies today, good communicators will normally choose the second approach. And it does not matter whether the audience is a group of highly-intelligent experts or whether it is made up of non-experts with an average level of intelligence.

Research has shown that however intelligent/academic someone is they prefer to receive their information in a simple way. This is reflected in the way that top newspapers and journals write today compared to 50 or even 20 years ago. And it is reflected in TED presentations, where the audiences may not be experts in the precise field of the presentation, but they are certainly experts in some area.

You may feel that this kind of simplicity goes against the rules of writing of your own language.

For example, Russian is a language that many Russians like to write in a complex way, where the meaning is not entirely clear until the end of a long sentence or long paragraph. Yet read this translation from a book written in Russian by two best-selling Russian authors – Maksim Ilyakhov and Ljudmila Sarycheva – advising fellow Russians on how to write their language:

> *The text should be simple. Simple – that is, expressed as simply as possible, without prejudice to the meaning. If the text can be simplified, it should be simplified. ... Simple does not mean primitive. The text may have a complex idea, and you can use terms and introduce complex concepts. But if a thought can be expressed simply, it must not be complicated. Even if you write for scientists. Even if your reader is a government official or an academic. There is not a single situation where it is best to express something in difficult language, when it could be expressed in simple language.**

* Translated from Russian using Google Translate and then adjusted by me.

The authors then stress how important it is to actually 'see the bad' (my translation) – meaning spotting those phrases that say nothing or contain a lot of redundancy.

The point is that whatever your native tongue is, it is ALWAYS possible to write in a simple way. And in any case, when you write or speak in English, there are NO disadvantages to writing and speaking in a simple way.

7.3 Using AI to derive an outline of a presentation from a script

A possible first step in preparing a presentation is to write notes on what you want to say. The reason for writing notes or a script first, rather than immediately starting on the slides, is that you want what you are going to say to be reflected in your slides, rather than your slides to dictate what you are going to say.

The process of writing notes and a script is described in detail in Chapter 3 of *Giving an Academic Presentation in English* (Springer, 2021).

This section suggests what to do when you have your script ready.

i) Ask the bot if the info contained is in the best order – the bot will then comment and suggest a structure for your slides, and possible slide headings.
ii) Use more than one bot so that you can get different suggestions.
iii) Ignore any advice you don't agree with.

So, let's imagine you already have a script ready. This script can be in your own language, this will give you more control and freedom to say exactly what you want to say. You can then submit this to automatic translation or to ChatGPT for correction (see Chapters 2–4 to learn how).

Let's imagine you have written a complete script, which begins as follows.

Slide 1 Twenty years ago, Bill Gates predicted that in the near future, every household would possess a robot, similarly to how they own personal computers. Since 2023, AI-driven innovations such as image generation, virtual music and videos have significantly reshaped our world, and now we don't even need to know how to speak English to write a paper!

Slide 2 But where are all these robots? To truly enter Gates' *Age of Robots*, robots need to evolve, transform, and expand in a similar way as natural systems. Consequently, robotic researchers are turning to nature for inspiration, aiming to design robots capable of functioning beyond factory settings, navigating real-world and unstructured environments, and unlocking new application possibilities.

Slide 3 I am eager to share three exciting breakthroughs that my team and I have …

First, start a new conversation with a chatbot and submit your script with the following **PROMPT**:

> **This is a script for a presentation at an international conference on plant-inspired robots. The audience are scientists with an interest in robots. Is the order that the information is presented the most logical, or do you think there could be a better order?**

ChatGPT first suggested that I make various changes. When prompted, it then provided a structure for eight slides: the first three are shown in the screenshot below.

Slide 1: Introduction

- Set the stage by discussing the vision of a robot-filled future inspired by Bill Gates' statement.
- Pose the question: Are we truly in the Age of Robots? Explain why not yet due to limitations in robotics technology.
- Introduce the concept of seeking new abilities for robots inspired by natural systems.

Slide 2: Learning from Nature

- Transition by emphasizing the significance of learning from nature in robotics.
- Highlight the skepticism faced when proposing plant-inspired robots.
- Discuss the valuable aspects of plants to imitate: locomotion, materials, sensing properties, and behavior.
- Introduce the idea of "plantoids" and the innovation they bring to the field of robotics.

Slide 3: Unveiling the Power of Roots

- Delve into the remarkable attributes of plant roots and their suitability for soil exploration.
- Explain why roots excel in extreme soil environments and their ability to overcome pressure.
- Highlight tropisms and their role in root behavior.
- Discuss how plants create networks and communicate with other organisms, laying the groundwork for plant-inspired robots.

Basically, the chatbot suggested

- the order of the slides
- slide titles (the first title – *Introduction* – needs to be replaced with something more meaningful and engaging for the audience)
- what to include in each slide

Different chatbots will give you different suggestions:

1. Slide 1: The opening slide could benefit from a clearer transition from the introduction to the main topic. Instead of abruptly stating, "So are we really in the Age of Robots? No, not yet," you could add a sentence or two to bridge the discussion about AI and robots to the focus on plant-inspired robots. For example, you could mention that despite the advancements in AI, robotics technologies still need to overcome certain limitations, leading researchers to explore new avenues inspired by nature.
2. Slide 2: Consider rephrasing the sentence, "Some years ago, as I was saying I proposed for the first time to use plants as a new model in robotics," to make it more concise and coherent. Additionally, you may want to introduce the term "plantoids" earlier in the presentation and explain its meaning when it is first mentioned.

On the basis of the chatbot's responses you can then modify your script so that it covers the points that the chatbots have raised. Obviously, you should ignore any advice that doesn't seem appropriate. But the bot is great at highlighting areas that you may not have thought of.

7.4 Generating a title from your script

The original title of the presentation mentioned in the previous subsection was: *Robots and Sustainability*. Based on the script, the chatbots I used came up with these alternative titles:

> **Plant-Inspired Robots: Unleashing Nature's Secrets for Autonomous and Adaptive Machines**
>
> **Harvesting Nature's Wisdom: Plant-Inspired Biorobotics for Autonomous Exploration and Sustainability**
>
> **From Roots to Robots: Innovations in Plant-Inspired Biorobotics for Autonomous Exploration and Sustainability**

Notice how all three titles are in two parts. A two-part title can be used in academic papers (see Chapter 5 in *Giving an Academic Presentation in English – Intermediate Level*, Springer, 2021), but is particularly useful in a presentation. The first part (*From Roots to Robots*) is designed to hook the audience in, i.e. to attract the attention of people at the conference who are undecided about which session to go to. The second part (*Innovations for …*) is the more technical description to enable the audience to understand exactly what you will be covering. The original title (*Robots and Sustainability*) performs neither of these two roles, it is far too generic.

You can even use a title to generate a script. I used the following **PROMPT**:

> **Generate a script for a presentation entitled: Plant inspired robots: unleashing nature's secrets for autonomous and adaptive machines.**

Below are the first few paragraphs that the chatbot generated:

Introduction

Good morning, everyone. I'm here today to talk to you about plant inspired robots. Plant inspired robots are robots that are designed to mimic the behavior of plants. Plants are able to survive and thrive in a variety of harsh environments, and they are able to adapt to changes in their surroundings. Plant inspired robots can be used to perform a variety of tasks, such as search and rescue, environmental monitoring, and agriculture.

In this presentation, I'm going to discuss the following:

- The inspiration behind plant inspired robots
- The challenges of designing plant inspired robots
- The potential applications of plant inspired robots

The Inspiration Behind Plant Inspired Robots

Plants are able to survive and thrive in a variety of harsh environments because they have evolved to be efficient and adaptable. They are able to collect energy from sunlight, water, and nutrients, and they are able to store energy for later use. Plants are also able to sense their surroundings and respond to changes in the environment.

You can use this approach when you are feeling uninspired and have no idea where to start. However, note that Germini's script is:

1. boringly standard, and unlikely to hook the audience in
2. incredibly generic, i.e. lacking specific examples, statistics, counter-intuitive information, anecdotes. Nevertheless, it is at least a potential starting point for you.

To learn about good introductions to a presentation see Chapters 6 and 7 in *Giving an Academic Presentation in English – Intermediate Level* (Springer, 2021).

7.5 Using a chatbot to make suggestions on images to use

Continuing the same chat as I had started earlier I gave ChatGPT the following **PROMPT**.

Could you now suggest what images I could include for each slide?

The chatbot then provided me with suggestions for every slide.

Certainly! While I can't directly insert images, I can suggest the types of images that would complement each slide of your presentation. You can find relevant images from scientific publications, online resources, or create your own visual aids to support your presentation.

Slide 1: Introduction

- Image: The cover of the July 2007 Scientific American featuring Bill Gates with a robot and a PC.
- Image: Visual representation of different types of robots and technology.

Slide 2: Learning from Nature

- Image: Comparison of different animals and plants to highlight the diversity of biological inspiration.
- Image: An iconic plant alongside an innovative robotic design.

Various AI-art applications can help you generate your own images. Also, PowerPoint's 'Design' feature can considerably increase the quality of your slides.

To learn about images for a presentation see Chapter 9 in *Giving an Academic Presentation in English* (Springer, 2021).

7.6 Using a chatbot 'to see the bad' and add 'the good' in your presentation script

A chatbot can help you considerably to 'see the bad' (see end of 7.1) in your presentation script. You can use the following prompts:

> **List the words and phrases that I can delete in the following extract from a presentation speech on xyz.**
>
> **What concepts could I remove in this extract from ...?**

But seeing and cutting the 'bad' is not enough. You also need to add the 'good', i.e. fill your script with useful information and examples.

AI can help:

> **What information is missing from ...?**
>
> **What example of an xyx could I give ...?**
>
> **What would you add to this speech on ...?**
>
> **If I am an non-expert, what additional information would help me understand this ...?**
>
> **Suggest 10 FAQs on the topic of xyz.**
>
> **Use bullets to list the five main take home points on the basis of this script for a presentation.**

7.7 Generating questions for your Q&A session

When I ask my PhD students which three aspects of giving a presentation at an international conference they fear the most, all of them include not understanding the questions in the Q&A session. To learn how to deal with this session see Chapter 9 in *Giving an Academic Presentation in English* (Springer, 2021).

Here, I am going to suggest two ways that AI can help you.

GET FRIENDS AND FAMILY TO GENERATE QUESTIONS

1. Show your presentations to as many different people as possible (not just fellow researchers, but also to non-experts among your friends and family). Get them to suggest questions that they would be interested in asking you about your work.
2. Translate their questions into English using machine translation, then submit it to a bot for correction.
3. Now use a text-to-speech application to listen to how these questions should be said. The idea is that if you practise listening to all the possible questions you may be asked, then you have a greater chance of hearing them and understanding them.

Note: If in any case you don't understand a question, admit it. Just say: Sorry, I am not sure I have understood your question. Please could you ask me at the coffee break.

USE A BOT TO GENERATE QUESTIONS

When you write a prompt for the chatbot to generate potential questions, make sure you specify what kind of audience. I asked a bot to generate questions for an audience of:

1. experts in biorobotics and related fields
2. non-expert scientists
3. 18 year old high schoolers who are studying biology at school

Here is one example each for the three audiences above:

1. *In terms of scalability, how feasible is it to deploy a large number of plantoid robots simultaneously for soil exploration or monitoring tasks?*
2. *How might these plant-inspired robots help in finding survivors in disaster scenarios, and how do they navigate through debris?*
3. *What role do you see plant-inspired robots playing in space exploration, and how might they help with anchoring structures?*

You might have already thought of many of the questions that the bot generates for you, but some will be new. Also, you can see that the three questions above are not substantially different from each other in terms of level of 'difficulty' despite your prompt to get the bot to produce questions for very different audiences. This doesn't matter because it is the content of the question that counts, not just in how it is constructed in English.

You can then

- integrate the answers to what you consider to be key questions within the main presentation
- exploit some of the other questions to create additional slides that you can use if someone asks you that specific question
- prepare answers for all the questions

You can then follow up with this **PROMPT**:

> **Now please answer the 10 questions that you have just provided for the 18-year olds.**

Below is the answer to one of the questions.

How do plants and their roots inspire the design of robots, and what makes roots so special for exploring soil? Plants and their roots serve as inspiration for designing robots because roots possess unique qualities that make them efficient at exploring soil. Roots are specialized structures that grow towards water and nutrients in the soil. This growth allows them to navigate through the complex underground environment. By mimicking the growth process of roots, scientists can create robots that can move through soil and explore different areas.

However, note how the explanation is rather academic. So you have to coax the bot to provide something more suitable:

> **OK, can you repeat the task, but this time in a more colloquial way.**

This provides a more suitable answer if, for example, you had to give a talk at a high school:

> **Scientists are checking out plants because they've got some nifty tricks we can use in making robots. Plant roots are awesome because they're like nature's underground explorers – they know how to dig around in the dirt and find all the good stuff.**

Check the bot's response. Change any words that you are not familiar with (e.g. *nifty*) because they might sound strange both to you and the audience if you use them.

7.8 AI for pronunciation

In 2023, HYBE, one of the largest music companies in South Korea, used AI technology to help its K-pop singer, MIDNATT sing in six different languages – English, Korean, Spanish, Japanese, Chinese and Vietnamese. MIDNATT, also known as Lee Hyun, only speaks limited English and Chinese in addition to Korean. He first recorded the song in each of the six languages with his imperfect pronunciation. The lyrics were then recorded by native speakers. AI did the rest by applying the native pronunciation to Lee's singing to make the singing sound totally authentic.

As the above example shows, there are a lot of tricks that you can do with AI. Check out the latest versions of the following types of technology:

- Text-to-speech: These convert your script into a sound file. You can choose the voice (gender, accent). You can then use the audio file to practise your speech.
- Simulating your own voice: With samples of your own voice you can train an app to read your script aloud. (You could even lip sync to the audio while giving your presentation!)
- Voice analysis: Such apps compare your voice quality and pronunciation with that of a native speaker. The apps are specifically designed for non-native speakers.
- Subtitling: If you are concerned that your online audience may not be able to understand your accent or pronunciation, you can use an app to automatically provide subtitles based on your script.

I have not mentioned these apps by name as at the time of writing there is a boom in such applications and it is difficult to know at this point which ones will emerge as leaders in the field.

A simple chatbot can help you with your presentation by indicating to you which words you might have difficulty in pronouncing. I inserted the following prompt:

> **I am an Indonesian. I have to give an oral presentation. Please indicate which words in the following text an Indonesian might have difficulty pronouncing in English. "A study by Donald McCabe conducted at Rutgers University (Newark, USA) showed that only 6% of professors report cheating regularly (54% rarely, 40% never). The study highlighted that in an era of political corruption, drug-taking athletes, and illegal downloading (of movies, music and books), students are not able to understand that cheating and plagiarism are wrong".**

The bot replied initially with a list of 10 words it thought that an Indonesian might have problems with. Here are the first four:

> ***Rutgers University**: Some Indonesians might find the combination of "Rutgers" and "University" challenging due to the specific sounds and syllable structure.*
>
> ***McCabe**: This name might be pronounced differently due to English phonetics.*
>
> ***professors**: The combination of "pro" and "fessors" might be tricky due to the "f" sound and the combination of consonants.*
>
> ***cheating**: The "ch" sound can be challenging for some Indonesian speakers.*

I followed up with this prompt:

> **OK, thank you, can you give me hints on how to pronounce them, and also give me a phonetic transcription.**

The bot returned:

> *Rutgers University: [ˈrʌtgərz ˌjuːnɪˈvɜːrsəti] "RUHT-guhrs" "yoo-nuh-VUHR-suh-tee"*
>
> *McCabe: [məˈkeɪb] "muh-KAYB"*
>
> *professors: [prəˈfɛsərz]: "pruh-FESS-uhrz"*
>
> *cheating: [ˈʧiːtɪŋ] "CHEE-ting"*

Notice how the bot has provided two types of pronunciation, the first is phonetic, the second is how to say it syllable by syllable. This second method seems to reflect the way a native-English speaking person might say the words. It is not particularly helpful to an Indonesian. I could not find a way to get the bot to give a transcription that would closely imitate the sounds as interpreted by the ears of an Indonesian.

In any case you can try the following prompt and see if it helps:

Provide an Indonesian-friendly transcription of the words.

Alternatively, you can give a prompt directly indicating which words you find hard. In the example below, the initial text is the prompt, and then the bot explains how, if you were an Iranian, you should try to pronounce the word.

I am Iranian. Act as a pronunciation guide for Farsi speakers of English. I will provide you with a list of words that I find difficult to pronounce. Respond with their pronunciations, without any translations. However, I want you to take into account that I am Iranian. So please point out any typical problems that an Iranian might have with these English words. Here are the first five words: business, candidate, definitely, genre, hierarchy.

Sure, I'd be happy to help! Here are the pronunciations for the five words you provided, along with some tips and notes for an Iranian speaker:

1. Business: /'bɪznəs/ (BIZ-nuhs)

- Note that the "s" at the end of the word is pronounced as a "z" sound. Also, the stress is on the first syllable.

2. Candidate: /'kændɪdət/ (KAN-dih-duht)

- The stress is on the first syllable, and the "d" and "t" sounds at the end of the word can be difficult for some Iranian speakers to differentiate. The "a" sound in the first syllable is pronounced like the "a" in "man."

Chapter 8
Email and other forms of correspondence

8.1 Introduction

Most of the examples given in this chapter refer to emails, but the guidelines given can be applied to any kind of written correspondence. A bot can help you to:

1. correct/paraphrase – see 2.8.
2. give you clear examples of where the language needs improving (2.7)
3. generate an email (including the subject line) from scratch
4. recommend changes to the content of an email that you have written yourself
5. generate replies to emails that you have received

This chapter deals points 3–5.

I suggest you i) only use a bot- generated email as a draft – not as a final version; ii) delete most of what the bot generates (or instruct it to limit itself to 25–20 words); iii) add something personal of your own; and iv) not worry about making mistakes in your English (unless it is a very important email such as an application for a job or summer school) – at least your mistakes make you seem human.

A. Wallwork, *AI-Assisted Writing and Presenting in English*, English for Academic Research, https://doi.org/10.1007/978-3-031-48147-5_8

For more details on writing emails see the companion volume in this series: *English for Academic Correspondence.* You should find the following chapters particularly useful: 1 Subject Lines, 2 Salutations, 3 Structuring the content, 4 Building a Relationship and Deciding the Level of Formality, 6 Requests and Replies, 7 Cover Letters, 12 Writing a Reply to the Reviewers' Reports, 13 Communicating with the Editor, 14 Useful phrases.

8.2 Prioritizing the importance of an email

Emails tend to written very rapidly due to time restraints and conflicting tasks. So it pays to prioritize which emails you do need to submit to the bot. Low priority emails are those where you are not trying to make a particular good impression because the recipient is someone with whom you are in frequent contact or someone anonymous (helpdesk, hotel reception). In such cases it is not essential that your English is perfect. You can probably save time by:

i) writing the email in your own language and then using Google Translate (see 3.3 for writing in a mixture of your own language and English)
ii) writing directly in English and then get the bot to correct it
iii) not bothering at all with AI, and simply write the email – for low priority emails, a few mistakes in your English are not likely to have a negative effects

On the other hand, some emails need to be written in accurate English, with a formal tone, and with information that is both concise and specific.

Examples of such emails are:

1. applications: jobs, funding, summer schools, lab positions, internships
2. accompanying letters: letters to editors accompanying your paper, cover letter for job application; if the recipient sees a poor quality email, they may think that the manuscript or the candidate is of equally poor quality
3. difficult emails: responding to bad news, to a conference where you were going to give a presentation but now find you can't

The first two cases are extremely important emails. In my opinion you should submit such emails and letters to a professional. By not having them checked you risk losing a key career opportunity.

If you don't have the time or money to use a professional service, then a bot may be able to provide you with info regarding the content, but still have to assess yourself whether this info is actually relevant and useful. You will need very specific prompts.

Sections 8.3–8.8 deal with using a bot to generate specific types of emails from scratch. I have removed the salutations at the beginnings and ends of the letter (see 8.11).

You should ONLY use the bot's output as a model / template for your own email or letter. You MUST adapt it, remove what is not necessary, and add specific details that are pertinent to you. This will make the emails sound less generic.

Note that a very common DRAWBACK is that when a bot generates an email it

1. writes far too much
2. is not good at generating specific examples and therefore sounds very generic and unconvincing
3. includes one or more very generic paragraphs that add no value for the reader
4. uses a structure that is easily identifiable as being generated by a chatbot

Consequently in Sections 8.3–8.8, I emphasize the risks of using a bot, not only the advantages.

8.3 Application for a summer school

Read the grey box at the end of 8.2 before reading the rest of this section.

Below is a **PROMPT** for writing an application for a summer school.

> **Write a letter. Application for summer school 'biorobotics and nature'. My position: second year, PhD in biology. My qualifications: MA in biotechnologies, specifically x, y and z. Give reasons for me wanting to attend. Give reasons why other people on the course might benefit if I attended the course. Note the letters x, y and z refer to very specific scientific disciplines. Formal tone, but not redundant.**

Below in the box is the bot's response.

In *italics* are words and phrases that I think are redundant, i.e. if you delete them it will make absolutely no difference to the overall effectiveness of your letter. In some cases you will need to slightly adjust the grammar or sentence structure to account for the deletions. Basically I suggest that you delete:

- most adjectives (they are either totally subjective or simply add no value)
- standard phrases that actually have no added value for the reader
- paragraphs that contain a lot of words but no substance (e.g. the penultimate paragraph in the email below)

I have <u>underlined</u> two phrases which are examples of how a bot often writes in an overly formal and pompous way.

I am writing to express my *strong* interest in attending the *upcoming* "Biorobotics and Nature" summer school, *as advertised.* As a second-year PhD candidate in Biology, specializing in *the intricacies of* biotechnologies, and possessing a *comprehensive* background in disciplines x, y, and z, I believe this program aligns perfectly with my academic pursuits and future aspirations.

My academic journey has been shaped by my Master of Arts degree in Biotechnologies, which has equipped me with a *profound* understanding of the interdisciplinary dynamics encompassed by x, y, and z. My research *pursuits* have centered around applying advanced techniques from these disciplines to explore novel ways of harnessing biological principles for technological innovation. *By participating in the "Biorobotics and Nature" summer school, I am confident that I can further augment my knowledge and competencies in the emerging field of biorobotics, where the amalgamation of biology and robotics presents an avenue of immense potential.*

There are compelling reasons that motivate my desire to attend this summer school. Firstly, the prospect of engaging with leading experts in biorobotics promises a unique opportunity for me to broaden my scientific horizons and refine my analytical skills. The curriculum's emphasis on integrating natural systems into robotic design and function aligns *harmoniously* with my *ongoing* research in harnessing biological mechanisms for *innovative* technological applications.

Furthermore, I believe my participation in the program can contribute *significantly* to the learning experience of fellow attendees. My *comprehensive* background in x, y, and z disciplines will enable me to engage in *constructive* discussions and share insights that bridge biological theories with the principles of robotics. *This cross-fertilization of ideas is likely to enrich the overall academic discourse and stimulate innovative thinking among participants from diverse backgrounds.*

In conclusion, I am enthusiastic about the prospect of participating in the "Biorobotics and Nature" summer school. This unique educational opportunity resonates deeply with my academic pursuits, and I am confident that my qualifications, experiences, and passion for interdisciplinary collaboration will make a positive contribution to the program. I eagerly anticipate the possibility of further discussing my application with the selection committee and being granted the privilege to partake in this intellectually stimulating journey.

Thank you for considering my application. I look forward to your response.

If you remove all the redundancy and pomposity from the cover letter, your reader will be able to quickly assess whether your CV is worth reading or not. In other words, if the cover letter is full of redundancy this may persuade the reader not to bother looking at your CV as you have already not met one of the requirements of any post you are looking for – precision and conciseness.

I suggest you also ADD some very specific examples of what you are doing in your research that could benefit from attending this particular school. Your aim is to differentiate yourself from the other candidates, so add anything personal that you can.

8.4 Cover letter for resume/CV – example 1

Read the box at the end of 8.2 before reading the rest of this section. This section should be read in conjunction with 8.5.

To get a bot to generate a letter is very simple. Give it the **PROMPT** below and paste in the relevant sections of your CV.

Write a cover letter to accompany my CV. Position applying for: xyz.

Below in the box is the letter generated by ChatGPT for the CV of a PhD student in Chemistry. I have highlighted in italics those parts that you could certainly remove – the numbers in brackets refer to the explanations given later in this section which explain why these sentences should be removed or how they should be reworded.

I am writing to express my keen interest in the position of [Position Title] at [Research Institute /Organization Name], as advertised [mention where you found the job posting or how you learned about the position]. Please find attached my curriculum vitae (CV) for your consideration.

With a 3-year post-graduate degree in Chemistry from the University of Pisa, where I graduated with full honors (110/110 cum laude), I have developed a solid foundation in the field of Chemistry, particularly in NMR theory and instrumentation. *My academic achievements include a thesis titled "Study of the interaction between small organic molecules and cell membrane models through NMR," which was supervised by Dr. Marco Borsacchi and Dr. Silvia Geppi* (1). This research allowed me to gain comprehensive knowledge of NMR techniques and their application in studying molecular interactions.

During my studies, I also completed a Bachelor of Sciences in Chemistry at the University of Pisa, graduating with full honors (110/110 cum laude). *My undergraduate thesis focused on the experimental determination and comparison of NMR parameters of Non-Linear Optical molecules, showcasing my proficiency in spectroscopic techniques such as IR, UV-Vis, and NMR* (2).

In addition to my academic background (3), I *possess* (4) practical experience in utilizing various instruments in a chemical laboratory, including IR, UV-Vis, and NMR spectrometers. I have a strong command of both solid-state and solution NMR techniques, both from an instrumental and software perspective. *Moreover, I am proficient in using the Microsoft Office suite and* LaTeX, *and I have excellent internet research skills.* (5)

Throughout my academic journey, I have demonstrated a strong team spirit and the ability to collaborate effectively with colleagues (6). My involvement in the scouts during university has honed my adaptability and integration skills in diverse situations. Furthermore, *I have actively engaged in extracurricular activities such as* teaching *dance and playing guitar* (7).

> *I am proud to have contributed to the scientific community as* a coauthor of an article published in the Journal of Physical Chemistry A, *titled "Integrated NMR and Computational Study of Push – Pull NLO Probes: Interplay of Solvent and Structural Effects." Additionally, I presented a poster on "The interaction between olive fruit fly (Bactrocera oleae) pheromone and phospholipidic membrane: a multinuclear investigation" at the XL National Congress on Magnetic Resonance.* (8).
>
> *To further enhance my skills and knowledge, I attended the NMR Basis School organized by Fondazione per le Biotecnologie, where I gained insights into instrumentations, spectra interpretation, and NMR theory. I also participated in the Solid-state NMR in pharmaceutics Workshop organized by the Italian Group of Magnetic Resonance Discussion (GIDRM).* (9)
>
> *I am confident that my academic achievements, practical skills, and passion for Chemistry make me a strong candidate for the [Position Title] role at [Company/Organization Name]. I am eager to contribute to your organization's objectives and collaborate with a team of dedicated professionals.* (10)
>
> *Thank you for considering my application. I would welcome the opportunity to discuss my qualifications further and elaborate on how my expertise aligns with the requirements of the position. I can be reached at your convenience via email at [Email Address] or by phone at [Phone Number].* (11)
>
> *I look forward to the possibility of discussing my application in more detail.* (12)

The biggest issue with the bot's letter is that it is too long – no one is going to read 528 words. In fact, they may not read the letter at all, and simply go straight to your CV. However, this accompanying letter may be a mandatory part of the job application process.

Let's look at my suggestions for deletion / replacement.

1) Instead of writing the title of your thesis (which may or may not be self-explanatory, write something more concise explaining what you did. There is no need to mention your tutors unless they are known personally to the person who will read your CV.
2) Your undergraduate thesis is fine to mention in the CV, but not in the letter – given that in this case the candidate is at a PhD level.
3) Delete phrases like this that add no value.
4) Prefer *have* to *possess*.
5) Again, fine for the CV, but you are trying to keep the cover letter short.
6) Avoid saying things that you cannot substantiate with clear evidence. This type of information is better put in a reference letter (e.g. a letter from your professor, or someone you have worked for).
7) Personal interests are not normally mentioned in a cover letter.

Note: In some cases ChatGPT may repeat grammatical mistakes that are found in the document you submitted. On her CV, the candidate wrote 'playing guitar' – the definite article is required here, so it should be 'playing the guitar'. This is another reason why it is so important to get your CV checked by a native speaker.

8–9) In the cover letter you don't need to be as specific as this. You could simply write: *I have written two papers, presented a poster at a conference, and attended a summer school on biotechnologies.*

10–12) These paragraphs make the cover letter unnecessarily long, occupy a lot of space, and contain no useful information. Also they sound as if they have been taken from a template entitled 'how to write a cover letter'. Everything you write must sound as if you personally wrote it.

8.5 Cover letter for resume/CV – example 2

One issue with the accompanying letter given in 8.4 is that it doesn't specify WHY you would be suitable for that particular post. An alternative solution is to include in your prompt the key parts of the text of the advertisement for the job you are applying for. If you are not responding to an advert, go on the institute's or company's website and try and understand what specific skills the people who work there have. Include a list of these skills in your **PROMPT**.

In the **PROMPT** below I have used CAPITAL LETTERS to help the bot understand what the key words are. Capital letters are the only formatting that ChatGPT currently accepts.

> **Write a cover letter. I have pasted my CV and a job description. Please write reasons why my qualifications match the job description. In CAPITAL LETTERS are the key points of the job description. Job description: "We have an exciting opportunity for a scientist to work in our talented science team helping to DEVELOP two of our SOFTWARE programs. These programs aim to identify and CONTROL IMPURITY and DEGRADANT FORMATION in PHARMACEUTICAL DRUG PRODUCTS to aid CHEMICAL SAFETY assessments. Your job will involve COLLECTING, CURATING, and ANALYSING data to develop 'rules' that will be embedded in the software. As such, you will be at the forefront of the scientific development of this software and can determine its direction and growth". My CV: xxxx**

As in the previous subsection (8.4) the bot produced a ridiculously long cover letter, again nearly 500 words. However it did try to find links between the CV and the job description.

Below in the box are the first three paragraphs of the bot's letter. To save space, I have removed some parts and replaced them with three dots (...).

The phrases highlighting the links between the CV and the job spec are <u>underlined</u>.

In *italics* are the words and phrases you could remove, including some parts that are also underlined. This is because you don't want to push your case too hard. If the recipient sees 'data collection and interpretation', they already know that this is a crucial skillset, so that they don't need you to tell them!

> I am writing to express my *strong* interest in the Scientist position within your *talented science* team, *as advertised in the job description.* With a solid academic background and hands-on experience in chemistry, particularly in the realm of NMR techniques and data analysis, I am excited about the prospect of contributing to the development of your software programs aimed at impurity and degradant formation analysis for pharmaceutical drug products.
>
> *During my academic journey*, ... I further pursued a postgraduate degree in Chemistry, with my thesis focusing on .... This research not only honed my analytical skills but also allowed me to grasp the intricate nuances of data collection and interpretation, *a skillset crucial for the successful development of your software programs*.
>
> Having coauthored research articles and presented posters ... I have firsthand experience in combining theoretical insights with practical experimentation. This exposure has equipped me with the proficiency to curate and analyze data effectively, *which aligns seamlessly with your requirement to develop 'rules' that will be integrated into your software*.

The bot wrote a total of seven paragraphs, but the last four were made up of a series of generic phrases that added no value to the reader. Remember that your cover letter is a reflection of you. You want to show the reader that you know what is relevant and what is not, and that you understand the importance of being concise and to the point.

If you compare the email above with the one in 8.4, you will notice that the bot tends to recycle the same phrases and words e.g. *academic journey, honed*. Readers, particularly in Human Resources departments, will spot such phrases and thus know you have generated your letter using a chatbot, which will probably reflect badly on you.

8.6 Request to a professor

I have received thousands of emails from my PhD students over the years. I have noticed that since the advent of ChatGPT, these emails have become unnecessarily longer and much more formal. The emails always have the same structure, the same unnecessary remarks, and the same soulless style. Here is an example of a student who wants to know whether I will be doing an online course this year.

> I hope this email finds you well.
>
> I am writing to follow up on a topic we discussed last year regarding the Scientific Writing course. I had previously inquired about the possibility of taking the course online due to certain constraints I faced, but at that time, online participation was not feasible.
>
> As the new academic year approaches, I was wondering if there have been any updates or changes regarding the availability of the course in an online format.
>
> I understand the challenges associated with adapting courses for online delivery while maintaining the quality of education. If there have been any developments in this regard, I would greatly appreciate any information you can provide.
>
> Thank you for your time and consideration. I look forward to your response and any insights you can share.

What kind of *insights* am I expected to provide? Why is teaching online *challenging?* It may have been in 2021, but not now. It would be easier for both parties if the email was short and simple:

> *By any chance are you doing your course online this year? My colleagues all say how useful it was.*

Here is another email with the overly formal and/or unnecessary phrases in italics.

> I am Andreina Marchesi, 2nd year PhD student at XYZ, and we met last year during your course "English for Writing and Presenting Research Work".
>
> I am writing to seek your *valuable* assistance in revising a paper *(the first one of my PhD journey*) that has recently undergone review *by a journal. While I am honored to have come to this point*, the reviewers have pointed out the need for a more academically formal style of English. *Given that you are a native speaker of the English language and you have an extensive experience in academic writing, I believe* your guidance and input would be invaluable in addressing this issue.
>
> *Your time is undoubtedly precious, and I understand if you are unable to directly engage in the revision process. However, even a brief glance at the paper or a few general suggestions would be immensely helpful.*
>
> *Thank you for your time and understanding. I eagerly await your response.*

All Andreina needed to say was:

> *I was a student of yours last year – I loved the course, thank you! I have a paper that needs revising. My department will pay for the revision. Would you be available to edit it by the end of this month?*

You will have noticed that the content/structure of the revised versions of the two emails is similar:

- State your connection to the person you are emailing (unless you are continuing a chain of previous emails). You don't need to mention your name.
- Say something nice, but sincere, about the person you are emailing.
- Say what you need from that person and give them all the info they need in order to be able to reply to you.

You don't have to mention all three points, and they don't have to be in the same order, but they are all that is needed.

When writing to your prof, I would say that you do NOT need AI to help you. Also, don't use a chatbot to generate an email that is in some way personal. In my experience, the bot will de-personalize everything and make it seem like you don't care.

Chatbots tend to fail to understand that most recipients in academia:

- Receive huge quantities of emails and have to prioritize which ones to respond to and in which order. Short ones that have a simple request, tend to get higher priority.
- Don't get beyond the first sentence. Instead in the email above the key info is in the third paragraph.
- Don't appreciate a series of standard phrases that mean nothing.

But if you do decide to use a chatbot to generate an email your prof (or anyone else) with a simple request, include the following in your **PROMPT**:

> **Limit the length to 15–20 words.**

8.7 Rebuttal letter

Imagine you receive the following letter from the editor.

> After careful evaluation of your paper, it has been accepted for publication with the following minor changes.
>
> i) In various sections of the paper, the English needs to be thoroughly checked for grammar issues.
> ii) The Introduction currently represents more than 50% of the paper, it should be reduced to no more than 30%.
> iii) The Discussion should end with a reflection on the limitations of the work.

A bot can generate a rebuttal letter.

> **Write reply to this letter from the editor. In each case ask why the changes have to be made:**

This generated a 313 word reply, which included queries such as:

> *Could you kindly provide more specific examples or areas where the grammar issues are most prevalent?*

The bot does exactly what you ask it to do. However, this is an example of a prompt that should never have been given. This is because it would have been much quicker and simpler if the author had done what the reviewer requested. By asking for clarification, you are delaying the publication of your paper.

The three points the reviewers made do not entail you re-doing experiments or writing a lot of text. i) It is likely that your English needs to be checked (if it has already been checked, then send the editor a certificate from the person who checked it. ii) Your introduction should never be half of the paper, so the reviewer's request is a good one and will certainly make your paper more accessible. Essentially, you just have to delete the redundancy. iii) All research work should refer to the limitations of the research. Again this is a reasonable request.

I recommend that in cases where the reviewers are not asking you to make radical changes, it would be better if you simply did what request rather than contesting them.

For a similar kind of email, see 9.13 in English for Writing Research Papers (2023).

8.8 Reacting to bad news

In cases where you feel you need to react to some bad news, e.g. a colleague's close relative has died, it may seem like a good option to use a bot to generate an email.

However a bot is likely to produce a very impersonal email where it is completely apparent that you have not taken the trouble to create one yourself.

In such cases, you should perhaps first think of alternatives to email, such as a WhatsApp that simply says 'sorry for your loss' (in the case of condolences).

If you opt for an AI generate email, you need to discourage the bot from being too creative and writing too much. You can use this **PROMPT**:

> **Write an email. Max. 50 words. The mother of a colleague who I do not know well has died.**

Below is the bot's response.

> Subject: Condolences on the Loss of Your Mother
>
> Dear [Colleague's Name],
>
> I am deeply saddened to hear about the loss of your mother. Please accept my heartfelt condolences during this difficult time.
>
> Sincerely,
> [Your Name]

If you don't give the bot a word limit it will produce over 100 words of trite phrases.

Other cases in my opinion where you do NOT need to enlist a bot's help are in replies to emails such as the following (your reply is in brackets).

> *I am sorry but I won't be able to ...* (OK, no problem)
>
> *I have had an accident and ... / I have to go to hospital and ...* (Very sorry to hear that, hope it was / is nothing too serious)
>
> *I regret to inform you that ...* (Thank you for letting me know).

8.9 Subject lines: specific but concise

Bots often don't generate a good subject line on the basis of your first prompt. You may need to coax the bot a little.

I prompted the bot to generate a subject for the following email:

> *I attended your presentation last week. I really enjoyed your talk – it was very interesting and also very pertinent to my field of research, which is hydro-energy robotics, i.e. water-powered robots. What I found particularly relevant, and which I think our two lines of research have in common, is ... Anyway, the reason I am writing is to ask if you could kindly give me the link to the online version.*

The bot generated 10 inappropriate subject lines including these:

> *Revisiting Your Captivating Presentation: Link to Online Version Request*
>
> *Link Request: Your Intriguing Presentation on Hydro-Energy Robotics*
>
> *Connecting After Your Engaging Talk: Seeking Online Presentation Link*
>
> *Remember Me from Your Presentation? Seeking Online Version Link*

The subject lines above are:

- too long
- contain unnecessary adjectives (*captivating, intriguing, engaging*)
- not specific – '*your presentation*', which one? Your recipient may have done several presentations recently
- absurd – '*remember me*'
- all have initial capital letters

So you may need to do more than one **PROMPT**. Try this one:

> **Generate a concise subject line for this email. Do not use initial upper case letters.**

This produced:

> *Link Request: Your Hydro-Energy Robotics Presentation*

The above subject line is perfect (except that the bot insisted on using initial capitalization!). Basically the entire message of the email is contained in the subject line. The recipient will know that they can deal with your request quickly, so this means that they will be motivated to open your mail and simply post in the link – without the need to write anything. Simplifying the recipient's task is a good way to ensure that you get a reply ... quickly.

8.10 A bot's good quality subject line is not necessarily an indicator of a good quality email

The bot is able to generate a good quality subject line even if the main text is not great, like the one below. So don't think that the bot's subject line reflects the good quality of the email that you submitted to it.

> *I'm Carla Giorgi, a PhD student from the University of Pisa, Italy. I'm the author of a paper at ISXC16. Yesterday, I booked my hotel room using the forms on ISXC16 website. I'm waiting to be contacted, as specified in the message after sending the form. Please could you tell me if there are some problems with my reservation, if it was not successful, and when I'll be contacted. I apologize for my scholastic English; I hope to clearly have explained my problem. Thanking you in advance, I look forward to hearing from you soon. Best regards, Carla Giorgi*

Carla's own subject line was 'Reservation inquiry'. Her subject line is not effective because it is written from HER point of view, not the recipient's. A hotel's mail inbox is full of reservation inquiries, so Giorgia's subject does not help the reception desk.

The bot's suggestion is much more useful, although the word 'hotel' could be deleted:

Hotel Reservation Inquiry for ISXC16 – Carla Giorgi

In this case, the bot's good subject line is not an indicator of a good quality email. In reality, Carla's email contains a lot of unnecessary details. Remember the less specific and pertinent your email is, the less likely the recipient will read it.

In Carla's case a simpler alternative is to get the bot to rewrite her email using one sentence. You need to specify a maximum number of words otherwise the bot may produce a 60-word sentence containing lots of commas and semicolons.

Please express this email in ONE simple sentence. 10 words max:

An even better solution in Carla's situation is to write the email herself in the most concise and simple format possible, for example:

I am going to ISXC16 conference. I made a hotel reservation (ref. 2434). I have had no reply.

The recipient, in this case, will not be offended by the brevity of your email, nor will they think it is strange that there are no salutations. In fact you have made their job much simpler by only giving them the info they need.

For more details on subject lines in emails see Chapter 1 in the companion volume in this series: *English for Academic Correspondence.*

8.11 Salutations

Salutations are what you find at the beginning and ends of emails e.g. *Dear Adrian ... Best regards.*

There is an effective and easy way to write salutations that does not require the help of AI. Just follow these guidelines.

Dear first name – if you know the person already and are on an equal level on a hierarchy, or because the recipient has specifically asked you to use their first name

Dear first name + last name – the first, and only the first, time you communicate with someone. When you get a reply, see how they sign themselves (i.e. just first name, or full name) and then use their form in your next email.

Dear Dr / Prof + last name – to someone in academia higher up the hierarchy than you. First time and all other times, until they ask you to stop!

Best regards – to end your email: This phrase is good for everyone at all times. Unless of course you are on a very friendly basis, in which case you could just repeat the salutation that your recipient typically uses to end their emails.

However, if you think it is necessary to use a different salutation from the ones suggested above, a bot can tell you if the salutation is appropriate or not. In such cases, I suggest that you submit not just the salutation itself, but the entire email to give the bot context. Use the following prompt:

Is 'Dear Sirs' an appropriate way to begin this email?

> *Dear Sirs,*
>
> *I am an enthusiastic and motivated 24 year-old Electronics Engineer with a special interest in RF. I have spent the last six months doing an internship at XTX Semiconductors Inc in Richmond. This internship was part of my Master's and regarded the characterization and modeling of a linear power amplifier for UMTS mobile handsets. While at XTX I studied linear power amplifier architectures and worked on RF measurements. I will be getting my Master's diploma in March next year. Thank you for your time and consideration.*
>
> *Best regards*
>
> *Kim Nyugen*

In this case the bot indicated that *Dear Sirs* was not appropriate because it was too generic and that it would be better to:

> *Address the recipient more specifically if possible. For example, "Dear Hiring Manager" or "To the Hiring Committee at [Company Name]".*

The bot's advice is good. But what the bot doesn't say is that:

- It would actually be better to find out the name of the Hiring Manager.
- *Dear Sirs* is not appropriate in most English-speaking countries outside India and Pakistan. Essentially, *sir* sounds archaic and more importantly it is sexist (i.e. it is directed only at men).

To learn that *Dear Sirs* was inappropriate you would have to give a very specific prompt:

Are there any occasions where "Dear Sirs" is appropriate?

The bot will inform you that: *"Dear Sirs" has become less common in modern business communication and ... ... can be seen as outdated and insensitive because it excludes individuals who do not identify as male.* This is clearly useful information and should discourage you from using *Dear Sirs* in the future.

For more details on salutations in emails see Chapter 1 in the companion volume in this series: *English for Academic Correspondence.*

8.12 Using standard phrases: machine translation

A high percentage of the content of emails is made up of standard phrases. Every language has certain phrases that generally have an equivalent in English but which CANNOT be translated literally. You need to be very aware of what these standard phrases are, and what their equivalents are in English.

Machine translation into English works best from very commonly spoken / translated languages, particularly the major European languages. It works so well in fact, that it would probably be quicker to write your emails in your own language, and then use AI to translate them.

If your language is not as common, you can also submit a mix of your language and English or automatic translation. So when you are sure of phrase in English you can write it directly in English. When you are not sure, you write it in your own language. Alternatively, write the main body of the text in your own language, but write any standard phrases directly in English. You can use the standard phrases listed in Chapter 14 of the companion volume *English for Academic Correspondence.*

To learn about the specific mistakes that machine translators tend to make when translating emails into English see 16.6 in *Grammar, Style, and Usage.*

8.13 Using standard phrases: chatbots

If you write your email directly in English, do not make literal translations into English of standard phrases typically used in your own language. The result may sound strange or even comical and thus unprofessional. So if you submit an email to a bot, ensure that you only use standard English phrases.

In general, English-speaking researchers in the West tend to be less deferential to their professors and use considerably fewer salutations at the end of an email. However, a bot will not automatically reduce the number of salutations you have written. Nor can a bot automatically tell you that the salutation you have used is correct but too formal. For example, an expression such as *Sincerely yours* that might be considered perfectly acceptable by Indian speakers of English sounds much too formal or even rather archaic to someone in the UK or US, where even *Yours sincerely* tends to be reserved for very formal letters. A much more typical salutation is *Best regards*, which works both in formal and more neutral situations.

8.14 Generating replies

When you receive an email that needs a reply, you may not know exactly what to say or may simply not have time to write it yourself. A bot is very handy in such situations.

Here are some **PROMPT**s for generating replies in various situations. In each case, you need to insert any emails in the chain that might be relevant. All the **PROMPT**s begin by instructing the bot to use a professional academic tone in their reply to an email that you insert into your prompt.

> **I am unable to accept their invitation to the conference. Invent some academic excuse.**

> **The time they suggest for the meeting is not convenient. Suggest 10.00 am CET next Friday.**

> **I am sorry to hear that they can't send me the data I requested before the end of next month. Invent reasons why I need the data by the end of this month.**

> **I am not interested in the collaboration they suggest. Invent reasons why.**

> **I cannot do what they request in their timeframe. I need at least three months. Give reasons why.**

Sometimes it is quicker to reply to an email by making comments inline. Below is an example. The comments are in capital letters, but in a real email, you would use normal script and maybe a different color.

> *Do you have a timeline for this writing?*

> *END OF NEXT MONTH, IF THAT'S OK WITH YOU.*

> *What's the weather like with you?*

> *IT'S PRETTY AWFUL ACTUALLY. RAIN EVERY DAY FOR THE LAST TEN DAYS. HOPE IT IS BETTER WITH YOU IN CAPETOWN!*

I have tried many different kinds of prompts to get a bot to comment inline, but it fails to understand what it has to do. It seems unable to distinguish the person who is replying from the person who wrote the original, even if the comments are in capital letters as above. If you have any solutions, please email me!

8.15 Changing the tone

The tone of your email – formal vs informal, neutral vs friendly, composed vs angry / hysterical – can make a huge impact on the impression you give to your recipient. If the email is work related, then you need to sound professional and not too direct or critical of the recipient's organization or the recipient themself.

In such cases you can write your email, let off steam (i.e. let your anger or frustration out), and NOT press send! Instead, you can get the bot to give your email a more professional tone.

The bot will dedramatize your original version by:

- using more professional and less direct language
- removing any extreme phrases
- removing bullet points that highlight how many criticisms you have made (or it may make a soft change, for example, *two points* to *couple of points*). Numbering points tends to make criticisms too direct. However, giving instructions using numbered bullets is obviously very useful
- adding some conclusive and conciliatory final phrases

Sometimes you write an angry email in a hurry. You press 'send' then you regret what you have done. You may even discover that your criticisms were not well founded. A bot can even help you with this situation, here is the type of prompt you could use.

> **I sent the following email to my editor. I now realise I was wrong. Please generate an apology.**

The bot will probably generate an overly long email, e.g. 250 words where 50 might be enough. But you can then remove all the redundant parts and make any other changes so that it fits your situation.

On other occasions you might want to change the tone for other reasons. Here are some **PROMPTS**:

> **Make this email sound more authoritative.**
>
> **This email is to my co-author, who is someone who I have never met but is an expert in our field. Make my request more convincing by using a more professional style.**
>
> **I think I sound a bit submissive in this email to my professor. Make me sound confident.**
>
> **This email is an excuse not to go to a meeting. Make my reason for not attending sound more credible.**

8.16 Discovering whether your email is effective or not

When you have an important email to write and if you do NOT have a native English speaker who can help you (this would be the ideal solution), then a bot might be able to give you some clues. I submitted Kim Nyugen's email (8.11) with the prompt below.

> **Is this an effective email? Please indicate areas for improvement. Do not paraphrase or rewrite. I want a list of recommendations.**

Note how the prompt also states what you do NOT want.

Amongst the bot's various recommendations were:

Enthusiasm and Motivation: While you mention your enthusiasm, consider adding a brief sentence explaining why you are enthusiastic about RF and electronics engineering.

Internship Details: You provide good details about your internship, but you could consider adding a sentence about a notable accomplishment or skill gained during the internship.

Relevance to Job: Include a sentence that clearly relates your internship experience to the role you are applying for or to the company's area of expertise.

Future Plans: Since you will be receiving your Master's diploma next year, consider adding a sentence about your future goals or how you plan to apply your skills after graduation.

Its recommendations are useful but fail to tell Kim that is not clear:

- who the email is addressed to
- what he wants

Does Kim want a job – if so, is he writing to the human resources manager? Is he applying to a summer school – if so, is he writing to the course organizer? It is not clear from the email he has written.

When you write an email, you should always address it to someone in particular. Recipients feel much more motivated to reply if they have been addressed in person. It makes them feel personally responsible. Find out the exact name of the person to write to – from the website or by telephoning directly.

The reason for your email should be clearly stated as early as possible in the email. So Kim could have begun his email like this:

I am interested in applying for the post of junior scientist advertised on your website.

Or:

I would like to apply for a placement in your summer school.

8.17 Understanding how your recipients will read your emails

Emails are famous for being misunderstood. A lot of the blame for this is attributed to the

- tone – the writer thought it was friendly (and used all the right emojis!), the recipient thought it was too direct or rude
- lack of clarity – the writer thought they were being clear, but the reader understood something different

Less focus tends to be given to the reader's expectations and the order that the reader will actually read the information given.

Generally speaking recipients

1. want the key info in the first line, which may be the only line they actually read
2. need to be alerted if you are making an uncommon request

With regard to the second case, I asked my production editor if it was OK for me to delete some paragraphs while proofreading my manuscript. Generally, authors want to add paragraphs rather than delete them. In fact in her reply she informed me that at this time of the production process, I could not add any further sentences. She had expected me to write 'add', so even though I wrote 'delete' she assumed that she had read 'add'.

Why is this important? Because no bot could help you with this, unless you gave it very strict prompts:

> **Ensure the info on X is contained in the first sentence. And repeat it in the last sentence.**
>
> **Ensure that the recipient will understand that I want to delete Y, not to add Y.**
>
> **Ensure the word DELETE remains in capital letters.**

Chapter 9
The added value of a professional editing/ translation service

9.1 Introduction

This chapter deals exclusively with research manuscripts. There are several reasons why you as a researcher might need to send your paper to a professional English language editing / translation service. This is because there are some areas where you should probably not rely exclusively on AI and not submit your paper directly to an international journal for publication.

The various sections of this section tell you:

- the problem area
- how you could possibly resolve the problem with AI
- the limits of AI
- what a professional editor can do that AI cannot do

Below are areas where a chatbot is RELIABLE. A bot generally:

- corrects grammar mistakes
- identifies where punctuation needs adding
- paraphrases and summarizes
- makes suggestions on improving content and style of your text
- makes phrases more concise
- transforms passive to active sentences

A. Wallwork, *AI-Assisted Writing and Presenting in English*, English for Academic Research, https://doi.org/10.1007/978-3-031-48147-5_9

On the other hand, here are some PROBLEM AREAS. A bot tends to:

- make too many changes
- make logical connections between paragraphs
- not follow the prompt consistently
- generate generic phrases
- be unable to reduce a text by specified number of words
- generate sentences of a similar length – no variation
- always use same structure when generating text

At the current state of the art in AI, and generally speaking, ONLY A HUMAN can

1. judge the overall quality of your text
2. restrict themselves to making only 'essential' changes i.e. in cases where you need the paper back in a matter of hours
3. identify ambiguity
4. warn about biased or non-gender neutral language
5. make your key findings stand out
6. tell you that you have written too much
7. inform you that you have made factual errors
8. resolve issues relating to the style guide of your chosen journal
9. identify cases where you have self-referenced in a misleading way
10. warn about plagiarism or potential negative comments by referees
11. warn you that you have made cultural references that will be difficult for readers outside your country to understand
12. alert you to predatory journals, fake editing services and fake conferences

This chapter outlines the benefits of using a professional editor or translator and covers the twelve points mentioned above.

9.2 Practical reasons for using a professional editor rather than relying AI

You can save a lot of money by using a chatbot, Curie and/or automatic translation rather than sending your paper to a professional. But here are some practical – non-linguistic – reasons why it might be 'safer' to send it to a professional after you have used AI to help you write the paper.

RESPONSIBILITY – You cannot be sure that AI will make the right changes or will not introduce mistakes. You may lack the confidence and time required to take full responsibility for the quality of your paper.

CLOSE DEADLINES – When a paper is accepted 'subject to revisions', the journal editor sets a deadline for receipt of the revisions. These revisions do not necessarily solely refer to linguistic changes, but also alterations to figures and tables, re-analysis of data, repetitions of experiments etc. You may simply not have time to work on the English aspect, so having sending your work to a professional editor will save you time, especially as such editors are used to working to very strict deadlines.

CERTIFICATE – a bot cannot give you a certificate to send to the journal to say that the work has been corrected by a native English speaking editing agency.

9.3 What linguistic changes do English-language editors typically make?

The main work of a language editor consists of the 12 points listed below:

1. correcting vocabulary, grammar, and punctuation errors
2. dividing up long sentences and restructuring them
3. removing redundancy
4. rewording sentences that use *he* and *he/she* as generic pronouns
5. removing ambiguity
6. replacing or deleting vague expressions
7. restructuring paragraphs, changing the order of information
8. clarifying and highlighting findings, and pointing out areas where it is not clear whether you did something or another research team
9. highlighting where information is missing (e.g. you have forgotten to mention the limitations of your study)

10 pointing out that you may have plagiarized your own or someone else's work
11 hedging phrases that are making very big claims
12 highlighting concepts that are you unique to your country / culture, and may thus not be readily understand by other nationalities

You can get a lot of help with all these points by referring to the index of this book and to the relevant chapters in these two companion books in the series.

English for Academic Research: Grammar, Usage and Style (points 1, 4)

English for Writing Research Papers (points 2–12)

However, a good professional editor or translator will be able to cover these issues as a routine part of their job.

9.4 Judging the quality of a written text

In addition to the points mentioned in 9.3, a professional language editor is better equipped than you (or even a native English speaker) to judge the quality of a text.

Look at the text below. Do you think it

1. is a translation into English from another language?
2. was generated by ChatGPT on the basis of prompts written by a non-native speaker?
3. has been edited by a professional English native speaking scientific editor?
4. was written in English by a native speaker of English?

VERSION 1 During the summer months, it will be necessary for me to process over 11,000 applications of awards for the next academic year. My awards staff will, therefore, be working under very considerable pressure during the period from June to October. In an endeavor to relieve this pressure, applicants are requested to refrain from writing, telephoning or calling for information about the progress of their application, unless the enquiry is absolutely essential. In this connection, it would also be helpful if, as a general rule, telephone calls and visits to the office during the months of August, September and October could please be restricted to the afternoon period from 2.00 p.m. to 5.00 p.m. Your cooperation in this respect will considerably help my Awards staff during the busy summer months.

Version 1 was written in 1982 and was part of a letter from a local council in England to students about educational grants. It was written in English by an English person. This style of verbose writing reflects the way many academic papers are written today. It was also once a very common style in English, but is no longer considered appropriate. A professional language editor will immediately be able to spot such a style and find ways to simplify it.

A language is not innately verbose or innately concise. The level of verbosity or conciseness is determined by the writer, not the language. A bot does not know this, most non-native researchers do not (in my opinion) know this, but a good language editor does.

Version 2, below, is a rewritten version of the first three sentences of Version 1. It was revised in 1982 by the Plain English Campaign, an organization that has successfully transformed the way official documents are written in English (https://www.plainenglish.co.uk/).

> VERSION 2 This summer my staff will consider over 11,000 applications of awards for the next academic year. They will be working under great pressure from June to October. So please do not write, telephone or call about the progress of your application, unless your enquiry is essential.

In Version 2 the Plain English Campaign have removed all the redundancy, divided up long sentences into shorter sentences, used simple phrasing, and rendered the text immediately easy to read.

In fact you can scan it, without reading every single word, and still understand the meaning. This is because the key words and the key information stand out of the text. In Version 1 you have to make much more effort to identify what is key and what is not.

This is what a professional editor can do for your paper.

If you submitted Version 1 to ChatGPT with the prompt:

Please make the following text more concise.

it will still produce a 129 word text, exactly the same number as the original, as it may simply paraphrase. To produce the short text in Version 3 below required a different **PROMPT**:

Reduce this text to less than 75 words.

VERSION 3 During the summer, I'll process 11,000+ applications for the next academic year, putting my staff under immense pressure from June to October. Please refrain from contacting us for updates unless essential.

Version 3 is in reality not much different from Version 2 (apart from using *I'll*, which is inappropriate, *we'll* would be better). But to get Version 3, you would have to already know that your text needed a massive reduction in length. You may or may not know this, but a professional certainly will know, and they will do this automatically as part of their revision process.

9.5 Key issues with chatbots

Using a chatbot effectively does require experience. You as a researcher simply may not have the skills or time to check the changes that a bot has made to your work. You could potentially resolve these two issues if there was a way to prompt the bot to make only 'necessary' corrections. Currently a bot:

1. often does too much correcting
2. is unable to provide a complete list of all the changes it has made, even if specifically prompted to do so
3. cannot differentiate between 'essential' and 'non-essential' – it has no idea what an essential correction consists of, even if you try to train it
4. loves to connect one sentence to another by preceding the second sentence with a link word such as *meanwhile* – it may do this even when there is no intended connection
5. may suddenly start ignoring your initial prompt (e.g. to correct a text) and start summarizing it instead, or putting everything in bullet points

***

I have tried all kinds of prompts to get the bot to limit the number or type of modifications. The following paragraphs describe some of the frustrations involved in using chatbots.

A bot is trained to recognize the most common patterns of particular sets of words. It cannot distinguish between a bad mistake and a small mistake, between an essential correction and a non-essential correction. In its own words:

I recognize grammatical mistakes based on the extensive training data I've been provided, which includes a wide variety of correct and incorrect sentences. During my training, I learned the patterns, structures, and rules of grammar from this data. When I encounter text, I compare it to the patterns I've learned. If the text deviates from those patterns in a way that resembles common grammatical errors, I can identify it as potentially incorrect.

This means that even if you insert what seem to be quite specific prompts, the bot will still be too zealous in its corrections. None of the three **PROMPTS** below work consistently.

Please review the text below and make only essential grammatical and vocabulary corrections. Do not exceed 10% change from the original text. Focus on maintaining the original meaning and structure as much as possible.

I am going to submit extracts from an academic paper. I only want you to make essential corrections of the English language. I repeat, only ESSENTIAL grammatical or vocabulary changes. Do NOT paraphrase. Do NOT make changes to introduce variation. Do NOT add bullets. Do NOT change the format. The changes you make must NOT represent more than 10% of the total text.

Would it help if I provided you with a list of 20 types of changes that you typically make but which I don't want you to make? Is it possible for you learn from this list? Please be realistic as I don't want to waste my time.

ChatGPT does not know which of the changes it makes are really necessary (i.e. the changes are made in order to correct a mistake) or are just more commonly accepted ways of saying the same thing but that the original was fine and could have been left as was. The bot also admits that it likes to introduce 'variation' by using synonyms and synonymous expressions. But these 'variations' can lead to more than 50% of a text being modified for no good reason.

You need to keep inserting the same command, and to keep checking that it is doing what you ask. It may do what you want for the first few texts you insert, then it just seems to 'forget' and start doing its own thing.

However sometimes a bot corrects very little or even nothing at all. It seems quite random: you can give it the same prompt twice on different occasions and it will do very different things.

The statement reported earlier in this section would seem to inspire confidence: *I recognize grammatical mistakes based on the extensive training data I've been provided, which includes a wide variety of correct and incorrect sentences.* It does recognize some mistakes, but doesn't necessarily do it consistently. It is not 'intelligent' in the same way a human is. It is just looking for a pattern, it doesn't actually understand the rules of grammar, even though it can give you an explanation of a grammatical rule. It's a bit like a parrot that can produce a perfect sentence in English (or whatever language) not because they understand how the sentence was constructed but just because they have rote learned it.

Although a bot can often do a surprisingly good job, it can also be quite random. An experienced human editor is consistent in the work they do and is thus more reliable and trustworthy than a bot.

9.6 Language-related issues

A human translator can help with points 2–12 listed in 9.3 and with improving the readability and quality of your text (9.4). This means that they can tell you where your manuscript needs improving – no machine translation service can help you with this. Taking into account some of the points, particularly 8–10, could mean the difference between your paper being accepted or rejected.

A translator may suggest that you first re-work your manuscript in your own language in order to considerably enhance the quality of your text. This is known as pre-editing, and the skills for resolving many of the points made in 9.3 are detailed in Chapter 3.

Below are seven areas where you need to be careful when using a machine translator, but which a professional translator can resolve relatively easily. They are also points that a professional language editor can help you with if you send them a version written in English.

VOCABULARY, SUBJECT-SPECIFIC TERMINOLOGY

When dealing with words that have multiple meanings, machine translators generally deduce the context and select the appropriate meaning based on word collocations. Nonetheless, it's essential to carefully confirm that GT has captured your intended meaning.

If the text contains specialized vocabulary related to a particular field, verify that the machine translator has correctly translated the technical terms. You can check with domain-specific resources or consult experts in the field if necessary. A machine translator's dictionaries are extensive but not exhaustive, so if an unfamiliar word is encountered, the term in the original language may be retained (a spell checker will normally identify such words).

FALSE FRIENDS

False friends are words that look similar but have different meanings. A bot is unlikely to know Below is a table of 20 false friends that occasionally cause problems in scientific papers, taken from the companion volume in this series *Grammar, Usage and Strategies: Intermediate Level.*

	MEANS	DOES NOT MEAN
accurate	correct in all details	comprehensive, thorough
actually	really, in reality	currently, at the moment
agenda	list of things to discuss	diary, note book
argument	heated discussion	subject, topic
assist	help	attend, participate, be present
biological	relating to organisms	organic, environmentally-friendly
coherent	logical and consistent, understandable	consistent
comfortable	allowing one to relax	convenient
consistent	always done in same way	coherent
control	exert power, regulate	check, verify
convenient	suitable, situated nearby	inexpensive
economical	not expensive to run	inexpensive
education	what you learn at school	upbringing (what you learn at home)
eventually	in the end (after some trouble)	if necessary, in the likely course of events
fabric	material, cloth	factory
proper	correct, suitable, right	own
realize	begin to understand	create, develop
sensible	reasonable, practical	sensitive
suggestive	making one think of, allusive	evocative, with interesting possibilities
territory	land under national jurisdiction	local area

CULTURAL REFERENCES

There are some aspects of life that are unique to a country and thus need to be explained. Such aspects include how a government / parliament is organized, the education system, religion, food, terms connected with a company's organogram, and geographical and political words connected to how the various parts of a country are subdivided. The problem is that the same word may be used in various countries, but not have the same meaning. One such example is *college*, which can be a synonym for *university* in British English, but a *private school* in Italian. Even within English-speaking countries, the same word may have a slightly different usage, e.g. a *county* in the UK is not the same as a *county* in the USA, and even within the same country *college* and *university* may be used interchangeably. For further examples see 9.0.

You also need to check that names of people, or brands or companies, have not inadvertently been translated.

SENTENCE, PARAGRAPH STRUCTURE AND OTHER POINTS

A chatbot does occasionally break up a very long paragraph into shorter paragraphs, but it cannot be relied upon to do so. A bot will not usually:

- spot that a sequence of sentences have all begun with *moreover*, *additionally*, *also* etc. In reality, such a sequence tends to reveal that the author is just recounting a random list of events or findings, and often a new paragraph might be required or at least a more logical connection between one sentence and another.
- shift words such as *thus, consequently* or *recently* from beginning of sentence to later in the sentence (i.e. the bot doesn't understand the importance of the first word in a sentence).
- usually switch to lower case letters at the beginning of full versions of acronyms that do not require initial capitalization, e.g. Wrong: *This requires a PIN (Personal Identification Number)*; Correct: *This requires a PIN (personal identification number).*
- know when *could* should be replaced with was able to, e.g. *We found that treatment during the night could restore normal pressure = night was able to restore.*

So be aware of the above issues. If you have any doubts, then consult a professional.

UNCOUNTABLE NOUNS

If you are translating from a major European language, you should find that automatic translators don't make many mistakes. However, one mistake they may make is with words that are countable in the source language, but are uncountable in English. The issue here is an automatic translator may produce a sentence like this:

> *Patients are encouraged to ask their doctors for advice. However, if they do not agree with them or fail to comply with them, then the doctor may still be liable for any health problems that the patients then encounter.*

In English *advice* is uncountable. However, in many languages *advice* is countable and can be used in the plural form in the source language. The word *advices* does not exist in English and most automatic translators will use the singular form,. But when it comes to the related pronoun, in the source language *them* will be used to refer back to *advice* when it is in the plural, not *it*. In the above example Google Translate cannot know that *them* in both cases refers to *advice* not *doctors*, so it will leave the plural pronoun.

TENSES

The conventions for what tenses to use in different sections of a paper sometimes differ depending on the language and the discipline. Make sure that tenses conform to how papers in the target journal of publication are written. This involves both downloading the instructions to the author, and also quickly scanning some past papers published by that journal.

WORD ORDER

If you are not translating from a major European language, then machine translators tend to make more grammatical mistakes, particular in terms of word order, i.e. the arrangement of nouns, verbs, adjectives, and adverbs in sentences. Again, one solution is to rearrange the words of the source language so that they reflect the order that they would be in English (see Chapter 2 in the companion volume *English for Writing Research Papers*, 2023). This will help the machine translator to produce the correct word order in English.

CONVENTIONS

Different languages differ in the way they:

- use acronyms in terms of initial capitalization, and whether acronyms can be made plural (e.g. *one PC*, *two PCs*)
- write numbers and dates – for instance, you need to check that numbers are written in words (not digits) if they appear at the beginning of a sentence, that centuries are not referred to using Roman numerals, and that dates are clear given that different countries have different systems
- use commas and decimal points in numbers

9.7 Decluttering – removing excess words and phrases

Imagine a teenager's bedroom. Stuff everywhere. Difficult to even see where the bed, the desk and the wardrobe are.

Think of the bed, desk and wardrobe as key items – the other stuff is "clutter" which gets in the way of the three key items. In terms of language editing, "decluttering" means getting rid of all the excess verbiage that prevents readers from quickly seeing the key words.

Look at the text below. The *italics* highlight sequences of non-key words, i.e. words that give the reader no key information.

Even though GC/MS and GC-C-IRMS *are the main techniques reported in the literature for the study of* organic residues, *recently, we have seen an increasing in the applications of* high-resolution mass spectrometry (HRMS) mainly coupled with liquid chromatography. *It provides the opportunity of performing* accurate mass measurements, *has shown its enormous capability to* distinguish isobaric compounds thanks to the determination of exact molecular mass and elemental composition. *In addition, when the instrumental asset makes it possible, the* interpretation of tandem mass spectra *allows the elucidation* of chemical structures, *even in the case of* isomers, *to be obtained.* [Word count: 97]

You may not see this as a problem. Your paper may well be accepted for publication in any case. Publication is obviously a good thing in the sense that you can mention it on your CV / resume. BUT just because your paper is published this does not mean it will be read; and if it is not read, it will never be cited in other people's papers. The number of citations your paper gets is key to your academic career.

A massive added value for you is that an experienced editor / translator has an innate instinct to limit the number of words in a sequence of non-key words. In the revised version below, the maximum sequence of non-key words is six, whereas it is twelve in the original.

> GC/MS and GC-C-IRMS *are the key techniques for studying* organic residues. *However*, high-resolution mass spectrometry (HRMS) *coupled with* liquid chromatography *is becoming more common. Through accurate mass measurements*, HRMS differentiates between isobaric compounds *by determining the* exact molecular mass and elemental composition. *In addition*, tandem mass spectra *can potentially reveal the underlying* chemical structures, *even for* isomers. [Word count: 57]

You should also notice that this revised de-cluttered version is much quicker to read, and the key words now stand out. This is not surprising given that 40 non-key words have been removed – but not a single key word has been cut. Readers are much more likely to spot the key words even if they are not reading with great attention.

In the original version the reader will quickly find that they are not gaining much information through the long sequences of non-key words – they will thus soon get into a habit of skipping phrases and training their eyes to find the meaty information. This training involves effort. The reader may soon decide that their effort is not worth it. So they stop reading. And if they stop reading, then you have totally failed in your mission to disseminate your research. This is why removing the clutter from your writing is essential.

9.8 Non language-related issues

Artificial intelligence CANNOT currently resolve the following non strictly linguistic issues:

- the misguided assumptions authors make
- factual errors
- unethical self-referencing
- overuse of acronyms
- lack of hedging

These five issues are covered below.

1. ASSUMPTIONS

Authors of papers often make assumptions about what their readers do and do not know. Below are four typical issues:

1. In the Introduction or Review of the Literature, authors frequently introduce the topic as if no one has ever heard of it before, e.g. explaining what climate change is (in a paper intended for a journal on the environment and sustainability), or the evolution of the Covid pandemic (for a medical journal).
2. Conversely, the authors may fail to explain a very technical term or the meaning of an acronym. They just assume readers will be familiar with them.
3. Some authors seem to think that the reader has direct access to their brains. For example, the authors may use two or three words that might seem to the reader to be synonyms (e.g. *highlight* vs *underscore*), but which to the authors (and ONLY to the authors) have a slightly different meaning (e.g. *highlight* – call attention to, *underscore* – emphasize). The assumption in this case is that the reader will intuitively know what different meanings the authors have attributed to these different terms. In other cases, the author may consider that the use synonyms follows the 'correct' style taught to them at school, and additionally avoids boring the audience (in my opinion it ends up confusing the audience) – see 3.8 for the problems of using synonyms for key words.
4. The authors use words like *this*, it, *they*, *them*, *the latter* when such words could refer to more than one preceding noun (see 13.7 in *English for Academic Research: Grammar, Usage and Style*, 2023). This can produce very ambiguous sentences.

2. FACTUAL ERRORS

A professional editor may be able to help you with factual errors. My colleagues and I have found mistakes with:

- historical dates
- the wrong nationalities attributed to people (e.g. a client had written that the famous English scientist Darwin was Scottish)
- misattributed quotations (i.e. a quote is attributed to the wrong author) and misquotations
- errors with regard to descriptions of where certain countries are located (e.g. saying that a country is part of one continent whereas in fact it is in a completely different part of the world)
- definitions, outdated terminology, and terms that mean different things in different countries

An AI tool is unlikely to flag such issues.

3. UNETHICAL SELF-REFERENCING

An unhealthily frequent issue that I come across as an editor, and which no AI can spot without very specific prompting, is self-referencing. This means within their own paper the authors cite another paper that someone in their research group has written and whose name may or may not appear in the list of authors of the current paper. By doing so, the authors justify (and gain credibility) for their aims, methods or findings by showing that other people in the literature have done the same thing. In my opinion this is misleading and unethical.

If you have deliberately or inadvertently self-referenced, then a good editor will be able to spot this. Let's imagine your name is Marchesi in a sentence like this.

> *We use a method developed in [Marchesi, 2024] with the following adjustments.*

If the reader or reviewer does not check the names of the authors of the paper, they may not realize that Marchesi is actually the author of the paper they are reading now. To the reader it seems like the author of the current paper is using a method developed by a completely different research group, whose method has already been published and acknowledged. Instead Marchesi is using the method of her own research group.

Slightly less problematic is:

> *We use a method developed in a previous paper [Marchesi, 2024] with the following adjustments.*

But the reader still cannot be sure the *previous paper* was written by the author of the paper they are reading now.

A good editor will modify the sentence to:

> *We use a method developed in our previous paper [Marchesi, 2024] with the following adjustments.*

Or if you are referring to a paper not written by yourself but by another member or previous member of your research team, the modification could be:

> *We use a method developed by our research team [Alvarez, 2019] with the following adjustments.*

You may think this is just a minor issue. However an attentive referee or editor may get very annoyed if they think you have been deceiving them in this way. There is nothing wrong with building on your previous research – you just have to be honest about it.

4. OVERUSE OF ACRONYMS AND ABBREVIATIONS

Acronyms help lazy writers to avoid having to continually type the same words again and again. But do acronyms help reviewers and above all readers?

Acronyms and abbreviations are fine if they are well established, such as WHO (World Health Organization), PRISMA (Preferred Reporting Items for Systematic Reviews and Meta-Analyses), ANOVA (analysis of variance), and N (nitrogen). However, if they are acronyms that you have invented or you are just to save you time, this will be annoying for the reader who has to keep going back to when these acronyms were first referenced.

The solution is to reintroduce the full forms at the beginning of each section of the paper in which they appear. The old 'rule' was that you just had to explain an acronym once. But this was based on pre-digital reading where readers tended to read with more attention and frequently started at the beginning of the paper and read in chronological order until the end. Today people do not read with much attention and certainly do not read in chronological order. So if you want a reader to understand an acronym, then you can no longer get away with just referring to it once. Each section (and possibly even each paragraph) of a paper needs to be self-standing, so that it can be understood even without reading the other parts of the paper.

5. HEDGING

Hedging entails anticipating possible opposition by your referees and readers by not saying things too assertively or directly.

> *Hedges are central to academic argument and are abundant in research articles. Because they withhold complete commitment to a proposition they imply that a claim is based on plausible reasoning rather than certain knowledge. This protects the writer against being proved wrong while recognizing alternative ideas on the subject.*
>
> Professor Ken Hyland, Director, Centre for Applied English Studies and Chair of Applied Linguistics, University of Hong Kong

A typical hedge is when you are making a big claim:

> *To the best of our knowledge, this is the first time that XYZ has been done.*

By inserting the initial phrase, you protect yourself from the fact that in reality XYZ may have actually been done before.

To understand the importance of hedging as a device for 'protecting' yourself see Chapter 10 in the 2016 edition of *English for Writing Research Papers*.

None of the above five points (factual errors, assumptions, self-referencing, overuse of acronyms, hedging) are likely to be identified by AI, but they will be by an experienced language editor.

9.9 Areas where human editors can make useful suggestions

A human editor can offer you a lot advice that a chatbot can't. Below are three areas why you might benefit from having a regular working collaboration with a professional editor.

ALERT YOU TO PREDATORY JOURNALS, FAKE EDITING SERVICES AND FAKE CONFERENCES

The number of predatory 'journals' has continued to mushroom thanks to the pressures put on researchers worldwide to publish or perish. There is also a booming business in fake conferences and fake editing agencies connected with publication. Many of the 'journal' 'editors' have substandard English, but nowadays it can be subtle enough that non-native speakers of English often don't detect it. You may not be aware of such 'services', but a good editing agency will be.

STYLE REQUIREMENTS

Some journals stipulate using an established style: APA, Chicago, ACS (American Chemical Society), MLA, and others. Some agencies offer a service that includes formatting your paper so that it conforms to a particular style.

BIASED LANGUAGE

A number of journals state that submissions with biased language will be returned. A professional agency can certainly help you with issues regarding people (gender, nationality, traits) and countries (location, economic status, history). To learn more about such issues see Chapter 10 *Personal Pronouns, Names, Titles* in *English for Academic Research: Grammar, Usage and Style* (2023 edn.).

9.10 Be transparent about your use of AI

Many journals have policies regarding the usage of AI and may require you to declare whether you have used it. Some journals require you to report such usage in the Acknowledgements.

My advice is absolutely NOT to write an entire paper using AI, but to use it to check the English of a paper you have already written.

There are, however, areas where I believe it is totally legitimate to get a bot to generate text for you, for example titles of papers (4.8). A clear well written title that contains the key words that really reflect the content of the paper benefits you (as search engines are more likely to index it correctly), the referees (they can get a quicker idea of the scope of your paper), and readers (who can decide whether your paper might be worth reading). AI can also help you in other areas by generating texts that you can use as a template or for inspiration regarding which elements of your research you need to mention or emphasize in particularly sections. Chapter 4 covers what you can do for instance with titles and abstracts.

If you want to learn what a bot can do in specific sections of a paper, see the following sections in the companion volume *English for Writing Research Papers* (2023 edn.): Introduction 14.10, Review of the Literature 15.9, Methods 16.2, Results 17.9, Discussion 18.12–13, Conclusions 19.3, 19.10.

But **NEVER** use AI to replace the main tasks that you (as an author) should do:

- selecting the literature to compare with your work
- interpreting and discussing your data
- drawing scientific conclusions

Although papers have been published that have credited ChatGPT (or another LLM) as a co-author, this is a rare event.

Note: Software applications that claim to be able to check whether a paper has been produced with an LLM exist, but only return the likelihood of whether it was or was not written by a human. In reality, a human (particular a native English speaking editor) can quickly see whether a paper or any other document was written using an LLM.

Chapter 10
For EAP teachers: How to use AI in the classroom

10.1 Introduction

What students can learn to do using AI, in particular chatbots and automatic translations, along with the pitfalls they may encounter and must absolutely be aware of, are detailed in the first nine chapters of this book.

From the point of view of English for Academic Purposes, chatbots are very good at:

- correcting the grammar and vocabulary in texts written in English by your students (Chapters 2 and 4)
- paraphrasing and summarizing your student's own texts or ones that they need to read and absorb Chapters 2 and 4)
- providing grammar and vocabulary explanations
- simulating dialogs in particular scenarios, such as work interviews (5.5–5.8)
- helping with generating oral presentations and slides (Chapter 7)
- generating emails and letters that students can use as templates for their own emails and letters (Chapter 7)

A. Wallwork, *AI-Assisted Writing and Presenting in English*, English for Academic Research, https://doi.org/10.1007/978-3-031-48147-5_10

There are three main ways you can help your students to use AI. You can teach them how to:

1. write prompts to submit to chatbots (Chapter 2) in order to achieve the tasks mentioned above (correcting, paraphrasing etc).
2. pre-edit texts in their own language for submission to machine translation (Chapter 3)
3. understand where a chatbot or machine translation cannot help – they can both help to produce correct English, but not necessarily a good quality text. You need to be able to teach them about readability and good style (1.9–1.11, 9.5, 10.6).

To learn about the above points, refer to the relevant sections that I have put in parentheses. You will be able to adapt many of the examples given in these sections to your students' specific needs. In 10.3 I talk about the experiments I have done with machine translation and ChatGPT, which then formed the basis for this book. Sections 10.4 and 10.5 expand on some of the points mentioned above. Then the rest of the chapter is made up of exercises for you to test out in the classroom. The exercises do NOT test the use of ChatGPT. This is because you can find many such exercises in the three exercise books of this *English for Academic Research* series. The 2024 editions of these three books of exercises also have new chapters listed below regarding the use of AI:

English for Academic Research: Grammar Exercises

29 Using AI to improve, correct and generate your emails

30 Using machine translation

English for Academic Research: Vocabulary Exercises

11 Chatbots for correcting and paraphrasing

12 Using AI for translating and paraphrasing

13 Using inclusive vocabulary

English for Academic Research: Writing Exercises

11 Using AI as an aid for writing papers

12 Using AI for writing emails and presentation scripts

13 Using machine translation

If you are teaching intermediate level students, then use the following books:

Writing an Academic Paper in English – Intermediate Level

Giving an Academic Presentation in English – Intermediate Level

Essential English Grammar and Communication Strategies – Intermediate Level

To learn more about how to teach EAP:

English for Academic Research: A Guide for Teachers.

Check out tefldiscussions.com. My team have created a huge number of materials (written and audio) designed to stimulate discussions even in the quietest of groups and with the most burnt-out teachers!

10.2 What you can I do with AI?

The changes in the way people learn and use English today are not always reflected in EAP materials. Typical tools that hundreds of millions students use every day, but whose features and functions are still not exploited in EAP coursebooks, include:

- ChatGPT, Copilot, Gemini, Poe, Claude etc
- Google Translate and DeepL, Google Scholar and the Google search engine
- Curie, Writefull
- ContextReverso, Linguee
- Quillbot
- Text to speech (e.g. Speechelo) and speech to text (e.g. Microsoft Word Dictate), plus all the other voice recognition/simulation tools
- Grammarly, Microsoft Word Editor, automatic correctors, spell checkers
- Subtitles in: YouTube, TED, PowerPoint

These tools are used by students – generally ineffectively – to:

- check the English of a sentence that they have written
- translate from their language into English (e.g. individual words, short phrases, emails, reports, research papers)
- paraphrase and repurpose a text found on the web (kids do this at high school, students at universities, and researchers and professors in their academic work)
- understand spoken English
- practise pronunciation

Typically, teachers and books pay much more attention to language production/practise rather than correcting / revising what students have produced. In typical EAP and ELT coursebooks, very little space is devoted to teaching students how to correct and edit their own work (written or oral).

Yet in other areas of production – manufacturing, software, movies – protocols are followed to avoid problems before even starting production, and then there is a massive effort in post-production (e.g. editing in movies, user-feedback for software). I think as teachers we could learn from these experiences, and the advent of AI gives us a chance to focus much more on correcting what the students already know, rather than constantly teaching them new stuff.

After attending one of my courses a Turkish student emailed me (the italics is mine):

> I text with my friends in English, I can make jokes in English and make everyone laugh, and I've completed a bachelor's and a Master's in English. However, writing in English has always been challenging. Especially when writing academic papers or when I need to email a professor.
>
> I was afraid of making grammatical mistakes or translating directly too literally from my mother tongue. For this reason, I started to translate *secretly* from my friends by first writing in Turkish and then using Google Translate. It was easier for me to correct the translations of Google Translate. *When I wrote directly in English, I was losing the content because I focused on the grammatical structure instead of focusing on the content.* When I focused on the content, I was losing grammar.
>
> *I was doing this in secret from my friends because of fear that they would see me as inadequate.*
>
> This went on until I joined your course. Receiving the advice of 'use google translate' from a native English speaker made me relieved. Now I don't hesitate to write my articles in Turkish. I have avoided wasting time. *There are other more serious problems in academia to worry about, rather than obsessing about English. The important thing is to convey your ideas accurately and clearly. How you do this is entirely up to you. Language is just a tool.*

This email highlights two key issues.

- Using Google Translate is still associated with cheating (as is ChatGPT), with taking the easy way out, and sometimes as being even unethical.
- As teachers we tend to think that our subject is the most important one for students, but as my student says, English learners have other more important things to do in their lives and English is merely a means to an end. It is not THE end. So anything that they can do to speed up the time they spend writing English is very much appreciated.

In any, students will NOT stop learning English if they use AI to help them – if anything AI acts more like a personal tutor, revealing to the student

- the typical mistakes that they personally make
- new ways to express the same thing – both in terms of individual words and in terms of rearranging the structure of their sentences
- how they could considerably reduce the amount they write and thus at the same time reduce the number of errors
- how to improve their pronunciation

10.3 Why should I teach students how to use machine translation?

In my 'experiments' involving PhD students, I observed that using Google Translate resulted in up to 30% fewer mistakes, and the accuracy of the translations was generally around 90% (even reaching 95% accuracy if the source text was well-written and pre-edited for use with Google Translate). To learn about pre-editing see Chapter 3.

These experiments took place over two courses. In the first course, students were taught how to write scientific papers without any mention of Google Translate (GT). As part of the course, students submitted assignments for correction, and I noted the number of mistakes made. In the second course, I introduced GT. The students first worked on their texts in their native language, Italian, trying to adhere to English style and rules. They then fed their pre-edited texts into GT and corrected the output. Additionally, the students collaborated, offering suggestions for improving each other's Italian and final English versions.

To assess the students' final versions, I compared them with their previous texts from the first course and with full papers sent to me for editing in prior years, written by the students and their professors. These preliminary experiments have convinced me that GT outperforms most non-professional translators, provided the GT-generated text is carefully checked for errors.

As a teacher, I recommend testing out GT. Don't be discouraged by past poor Google translations or any difficulties you've experienced while translating from English into other languages. GT performs best when translating technical texts from European languages into English. However, I have also tested it with Arabic, Chinese, and Japanese. GT produces satisfactory results if the source texts are clear and straightforward. But, I reiterate, GT's performance is superior when translating into English, not from English. Additionally, the more technical the text, the better the translation. I advise against using GT for translating colloquial English and complex emails.

10.4 What you'd love to do with a chatbot but can't

ChatGPT, Copilot, Gemini etc do a lot of great things, which are outlined in the first eight chapters of this book. But they can't do a whole series of very basic things. Below are some examples.

You can insert a text and tell it to paraphrase all of the text apart from the verbs. In reality, it will paraphrase everything. You can then ask it whether it can in fact identify a verb. It can. It will provide a list of all the verbs in a text. You can then say: *Well, given that you have identified all the verbs, can you now paraphrase all the text but not the verbs.* It will then paraphrase everything again!

Likewise, although a bot can give you a definition and examples of 'essential information' or 'essential changes', if you ask it to correct a text but only to *make essential changes*, it will in reality have no idea what you are talking about. When paraphrasing or correcting a text, it cannot distinguish an essential change (e.g. *she study hardly* vs *she studies hard*) from a non-essential change, for example it may change *she studies hard* to *she studies arduously*, i.e. a pointless rather than essential change.

It can't do what for teachers would be useful changes in order to create exercises. For example, without multiple follow-up prompts, you cannot instruct a bot to:

> **Please put all the verbs into the infinitive form and place them between parentheses..**
>
> **Please replace all the articles (i.e. *the, a*) in this text with _______.**
>
> **Please replace each occurrence of 'a' and 'the' with 'a/the'.**

The problem is either the bot will totally misunderstand, or will only partially do what you ask (i.e. put some but not all of the verbs into the infinitive form).

But just because a bot is limited in some ways, it doesn't mean that it doesn't excel in others (1.2). So it is certainly worth investing your time in learning what it can do and passing on this information to your students. I strongly believe that it will add a new and useful element to your lessons, and is definitely something your students need and will appreciate.

See Chapter 9 for more things that AI struggles with but which a human has few problems with.

The rest of this chapter contains:

- Ten exercises that you can adopt for a classes of university students
- One exercise that is suitable for a General English.
- Three suggestions of other ways you can practise and/or talk about AI tools with your students.

The exercises are shaded in grey.

10.5 General discussion

The following three exercises (Exercises 1–4) are designed for you to understand how tech savvy your students are. The aim is for students to realise just how many helpful tools there are out there and that possibly they are not using them in the most effective way possible.

EXERCISE 1 Which of the following tools do you use? Rate them from 0 (useless) to 3 (excellent)

ChatGPT, Gemini, Copilot etc

Google/Yahoo search engine

Google Scholar

Google Translate

DeepL

Reverso, Linguee, Ludwig

WordReference and other online dictionaries

Grammarly, QuillBot, Writefull, Curie

Word's Editor function

Word's Dictate function

PowerPoint's Rehearse with Coach function

Quora

Text-to-speech apps

EXERCISE 2 Choose the most appropriate answer for you.

1. When I have used ChatGPT to check my English, I have found it to be:

a) very accurate and useful b) reasonably accurate and useful c) not useful at all

2. When I submit a text for review by Grammarly, I assume that it will find:

a) about 80–90% of my mistakes b) 60% 80% c) less than 60%

3. I use Google Translate to:

a) check a phrase or word that I have written in English b) only as a translation tool

4. I use the Google search engine to check the accuracy of a phrase, or use of a preposition etc.

a) Yes, and based on the number of hits, I decide if the phrase is correct or not b) Yes, but I check that the sites are .com, .co.uk, .edu etc

5. I think that the spell checking functions provided by Microsoft Office, Libre Office etc are:

a) totally reliable if I use the right settings b) occasionally unreliable even with the right settings

6. I use the various practice/rehearsal functions of slide presentation programs

a) never b) occasionally c) frequently d) I didn't know they existed

7. a bot to translate or correct texts is

a) a form of cheating b) dangerous because it makes terrible mistakes c) 95% accurate if used correctly

8. I use various tools to check my pronunciation (of individual words as well as speeches that I have prepared. In particular I use:

a) Word Reference b) Google Translate c) Speechelo, Lovo, Murf, WellSaid d) Adobe Read Out Loud

EXERCISE 3

1. Which AI tools would you use to check the accuracy of the following phrase:

   These informations are ...

2. Now look at the four screenshots below. Which tool/method seems to work the best?

TOOL 1

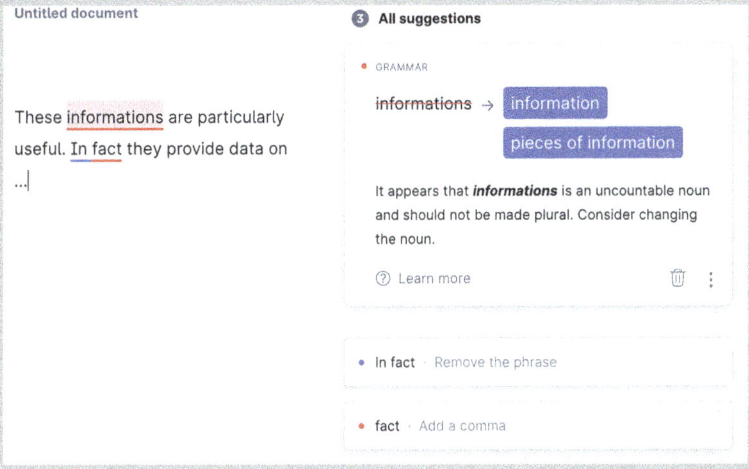
Untitled document
These informations are particularly useful. In fact they provide data on ...
All suggestions
GRAMMAR
informations
information
pieces of information
It appears that informations is an uncountable noun and should not be made plural. Consider changing the noun.
Learn more
In fact · Remove the phrase
fact · Add a comma

TOOL 2

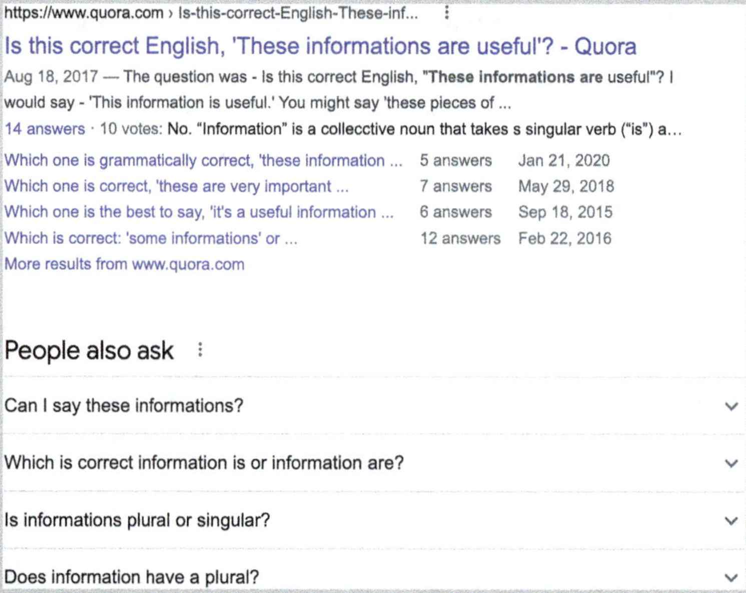
https://www.quora.com › Is-this-correct-English-These-inf...

Is this correct English, 'These informations are useful'? - Quora

Aug 18, 2017 — The question was - Is this correct English, **"These informations are** useful"? I would say - 'This information is useful.' You might say 'these pieces of ...

14 answers · 10 votes: No. "Information" is a collecctive noun that takes s singular verb ("is") a...

Which one is grammatically correct, 'these information ...	5 answers	Jan 21, 2020
Which one is correct, 'these are very important ...	7 answers	May 29, 2018
Which one is the best to say, 'it's a useful information ...	6 answers	Sep 18, 2015
Which is correct: 'some informations' or ...	12 answers	Feb 22, 2016

More results from www.quora.com

People also ask

Can I say these informations?

Which is correct information is or information are?

Is informations plural or singular?

Does information have a plural?

TOOL 3

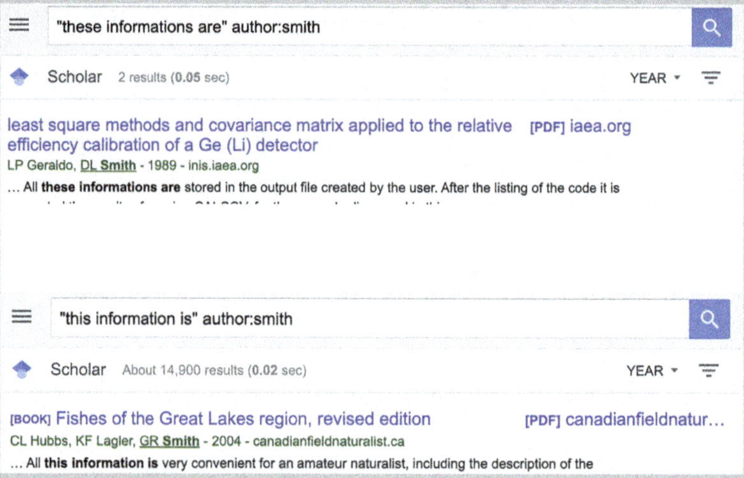
"these informations are" author:smith

Scholar 2 results (**0.05** sec) YEAR

least square methods and covariance matrix applied to the relative efficiency calibration of a Ge (Li) detector [PDF] iaea.org

LP Geraldo, DL Smith - 1989 - inis.iaea.org

... All **these informations are** stored in the output file created by the user. After the listing of the code it is

"this information is" author:smith

Scholar About 14,900 results (**0.02** sec) YEAR

[BOOK] Fishes of the Great Lakes region, revised edition [PDF] canadianfieldnatur…

CL Hubbs, KF Lagler, GR Smith - 2004 - canadianfieldnaturalist.ca

... All **this information is** very convenient for an amateur naturalist, including the description of the

TOOL 4

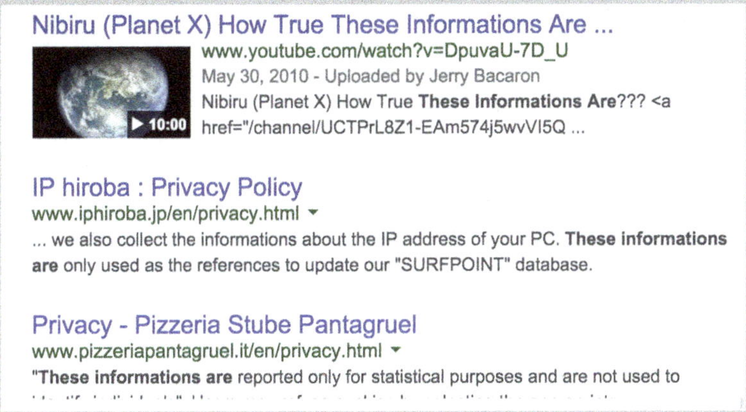

Nibiru (Planet X) How True These Informations Are ...
www.youtube.com/watch?v=DpuvaU-7D_U
May 30, 2010 - Uploaded by Jerry Bacaron
Nibiru (Planet X) How True **These Informations Are**??? <a href="/channel/UCTPrL8Z1-EAm574j5wvVI5Q ...

IP hiroba : Privacy Policy
www.iphiroba.jp/en/privacy.html
... we also collect the informations about the IP address of your PC. **These informations are** only used as the references to update our "SURFPOINT" database.

Privacy - Pizzeria Stube Pantagruel
www.pizzeriapantagruel.it/en/privacy.html
"**These informations are** reported only for statistical purposes and are not used to

10.6 Grammar check

The next three exercises (4–6) focus on grammar issues. The exercises that use jokes (5) and ambiguity (6) as examples of ways to present the issues that arise from using AI tools but without making direct reference to those tools. This is because they deal with problems that existed before the advent of AI tools, but which AI tools have subsequently had to deal with.

Exercise 4: Most languages use the present tense where we use the present perfect to express the concept of *I arrived yesterday and I am still here now*. Often students use GT to check their English. This is a dangerous solution (Point 2) as the translated version is correct in their own language, which makes the student think that the English version must be correct too. This exercise highlights the dangers of using GT to check the correctness of a sentence in English. Points 3 and 4 highlight the importance of looking at the number of returns as an indicator of the reliability of a sentence being correct or not.

EXERCISE 4 This exercises shows you the dangers of using Google Translate (GT) to check your English (rather than for its intended purpose: translation).

1. Is this sentence correct? *I am here since yesterday* (S1).
2. Using Google Translate (GT), translate S1 into your own language. Is the translated sentence in your own language correct?
3. Do a Google search of S1 (remember to put it in "quotes"). How many returns do you get? Is this number a very high number? What do you notice about the urls?
4. In your own language write what you think is the equivalent of S1. Translate your sentence into English using GT. Is it the same sentence as GT produced in Point 2?
5. Assuming that S1 might be incorrect, what other tense/s could be used in its place? What tense do we often find associated with *since*?
6. Repeat Points 2–4 using *I have been here since yesterday.*
7. What have you learned from this exercise?

Exercise 5: The joke in the exercise is not actually a translation. But the point it makes is a key one. In class, we often get students to correct each other's work. One issue is that a student may find a mistake in their classmate's work that is not actually a mistake. The same happens with GT, i.e. students identify mistakes in a GT translation that are not actually mistakes. In the case of this particular exercise, students may think that the pronoun *them* should be *him* or *him/her*. Jokes can easily be manipulated to make all kinds of grammar and vocabulary points. Jokes also make grammar and vocabulary exercises less heavy.

EXERCISE 5 This joke has been automatically translated from the original language. Are there any mistakes?

Secretary: Doctor, there's an invisible person in the waiting room.

Doctor: Tell them I can't see them.

Exercise 6: One of my jobs is being a scientific editor. I read research papers written in English by non-native speakers. Ambiguity is a big problem. The examples shown in this exercise were not taken from research papers nor were they produced by GT. But they highlight one area of ambiguity – word order – that students and GT make. I also think that it is important to inject some humor into lessons: EAP books can be very dry.

EXERCISE 6 The phrases below are ambiguous, i.e. they have more than one possible interpretation. Rewrite the sentences so that the meaning is clear.

1. They delivered food to the elderly residents living locally in a large box.
2. Like his mother, he had dark brown hair, with enormous black eyebrows, a moustache and a short beard.
3. If you take your dog in the car don't let him hang out of a window while driving.

10.7 Microsoft Office: Spelling check, PowerPoint 'Rehearse with coach'

The next two exercises (7 and 8) are designed to highlight the utility, but also the limitations, of two functions provided by Microsoft Office. Our students cannot possibly be aware of such failings. However, their attention needs to be drawn to such limitations otherwise they might be under the illusion that their work is much better than it is in reality. And of course solutions to these problems need to be suggested and practiced.

Exercise 7: Students may think that spell checking tools are fool proof – but as this exercise proves such tools have major problems with homonyms.

EXERCISE 7 Microsoft Word has found various mistakes in the following text. The four words underlined in blue are ones that Word presumes have been spelt incorrectly, though the word themselves do exist (e.g. *thanks* not *tanks*, which are armored vehicles). Now see if you can find the 11 words that Word has missed!

> Tanks for your male, it was nice to here form you. I was glad to no that you are steel whit the Instituted of Engineering and that they still sue that tool that I made for them, do they need any spare prats for it? I am filling quite tried, tough fortunately tomorrow I'm going a way for tow weeks—I have reversed a residents in the Bahamas!

Below is the same text, but this time submitted to Grammarly. In this case, Grammarly has found more potential errors than Word. In Ex 2 did you spot the words that Grammarly has underlined in red?

Tanks for your male, it was nice to here form you. I was glad to no that you are steel whit the Instituted of Engineering and that they still sue that tool that I made for them, do they need any spare prats for it? I am filling quite tried, tough fortunately tomorrow I'm going a way for tow weeks—I have reversed a residents in the Bahamas!

1. Check with the key to see which words both Grammarly and Word have missed.

   Key (words missed by Word and Grammarly are in bold): thanks, **mail**, hear from, know, **still, with**, Institute, **use**, part, **feeling**, tired, two, **reserved**, residence.

Exercise 8: PowerPoint's *Research with Coach* simply does not do what it says it can – your students need to be aware of this otherwise that they might use a script that PowerPoint deems as suitably interesting, varied etc, but which in fact isn't.

EXERCISE 8

1. Do you know the feature in the screenshot below? What do imagine it might be able to help you with?

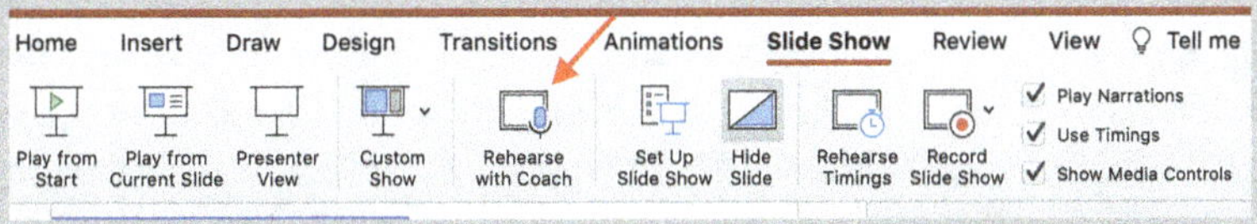

2. Imagine you have used the *Research with Coach* functionality of Microsoft Word to practise reading aloud the script of your presentation. The coach has generated the report below. Does the report appear to indicate that you did a good job in terms of content, delivery and pronunciation?

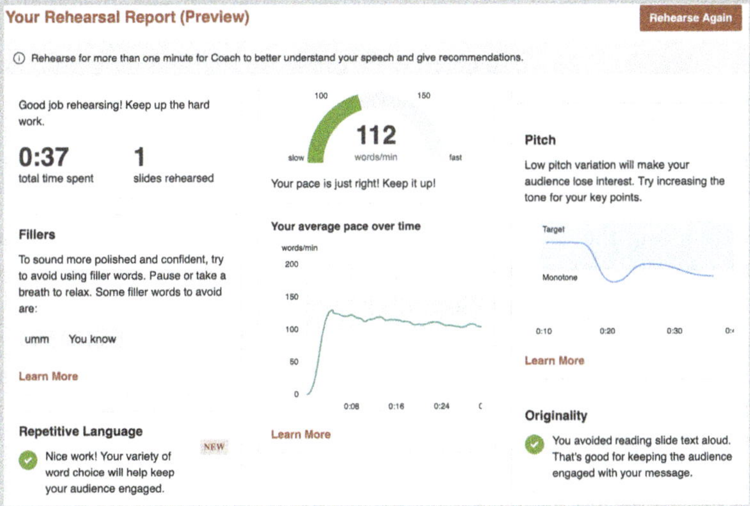

3. Based on the report above decide if the following are true or false.

a) You have used words such as *erm, um, you know, like*. Such words give the audience no information and could be annoying to listen to.
b) Your voice was rather boring. This could send the audience to sleep!
c) Your vocabulary was varied. This makes your presentation more interesting to listen to.
d) You didn't read word for word what was on your slide, which is not recommended during a presentation.

Key a + b: true, c + d: possibly true. In reality *Research with Coach* often fails to detect whether your vocabulary is varied and whether you repeated what is one your slide. In summary, *Research with Coach* is good at highlighting fillers, and analyzing and pitch, but not the other factors in its report.

10.8 Manual translation vs automatic translation

My experiments (see 10.3) with PhD students and computer scientists over the last 15 years have proved that the best way to improve the accuracy of Google Translate is for students to work on the source text rather than solely the text outputted by GT. Students obviously have far more control over their own language and can easily modify it.

Exercise 9 is designed to show students how long it takes to do a manual translation, and that a manual translation is likely to have more mistakes than an automatic translation. The translation the students are required to do is of Art. 18 of the Declaration of Human Rights, which is less than 50 words (in the English version). When students read the English version you should point out that the version currently on the UN's website includes the phrase: *freedom to change <u>his</u> religion or belief.* This use of *his* is no longer acceptable, and should be *their*. When students use Google Translate to translate the version of their language into English, they will see that Google too uses 'his' To learn more about the use of pronouns, see Chapter 10 in *English for Academic Research: Grammar, Usage and Style* (2023 edition).

Note: Given that the Declaration of Human Rights is such a common text, this exercise is not a true reflection of reality. In fact, Article 18 has been translated so many times into so many languages, that Google Translate probably just uses a stored version. So it would be useful to try the exercise with other texts, to see if they too work as effectively. I chose Article 18 as it works well in any class made up of any different nationalities. If you have a monolingual class, you will have many other more realistic options.

EXERCISE 9

a) Find *Article 18* of the Declaration of Human Rights in YOUR language (https://www.un.org/).

b) Translate it manually into English. It is only 47 words in English, so it shouldn't take you too long!

c) Compare your version with the correct version on the UN website. Note any mistakes you made in your translation.

d) Paste the original version in your language into Google Translate and compare Google's translation with your English version. Whose version is more accurate, yours or Google's?

Exercise 10 practices manipulating the source text by removing unnecessary words and phrases. The idea is to prove to students that the less text they input, the fewer mistakes in output. It is thus prudent for them to pare their text down in their own language before submitting it to machine translation.

EXERCISE 10 Choose any text that you have written in your own language of around 100 words. The text could be part of an essay or report, or an email, or a speech for a presentation.

- Without making any modifications to the text, use Google Translate.
- Count the number of errors that you think GT has made.
- Go back to your original text in your own language. Delete any words and phrases that are not strictly necessary.
- Insert the new text into GT. Count the number of errors.
- You will notice that there are fewer errors in GT's second version. Try to correct the errors that you have identified.

10.9 Example of an exercise not designed for EAP but for general English

The five texts in the next exercise were lifted directly from the web and are real examples of what happens if you simply cut and paste a text into Google Translate and press 'translate' and make no subsequent corrections. In reality, with a few tricks, GT can produce a much better version (see Chapter 3).

GT exercises bring to the fore problems that ELT books:

- already deal with e.g. correcting the English of texts, vocabulary, grammar
- sometimes deal with (but not sufficiently) e.g. word order
- rarely deal with e.g. removing redundancy, modifying unclear (or possibly incorrect) phrases through paraphrasing
- probably never deal with e.g. use of *he* as a generic pronoun – although this problem may frequently come up in class, it is unlikely to come up naturally in a reading text or listening exercise
- never touch – dealing with apparent nonsense (i.e. phrases that *may* have made sense in the original language but which GT has failed to render in English).

GT exercises thus cover both conventional areas of English usage plus totally new areas.

Another area that using GT brings up is paraphrasing, as in the exercise for Texts 4 and 5. Highschool kids and university students today spend a lot of time rejigging texts they have found on the internet and making them seem as if they had written them themselves. There is an art to doing this and although we may consider such an exercise as a form of plagiarism / cheating, the process it involves is extremely useful for students to learn. It involves understanding the text, choosing the best synonyms, changing the word order, switching from active to passive, or totally changing the phrase but without changing the meaning. It is a skill (paraphrasing) that I have rarely seen taught in coursebooks, but is a fundamental aspect of modern life.

Below are some thoughts on friendship written by people of various nationalities. Which two do you agree with the most? Why? [Ignore the italics]

1) A friend does not ask you to change, *he* does not judge your actions but at the same time *he* points out if you are taking the wrong path. You can confide thoughts, ideas, secrets to a friend; you can ask a friend for help without *them* asking for anything in return. (Italy)

2) Friendship is one of the highest human relationships, especially if friendship is based on honesty, clarity and love, as having a true friend in a person's life is very necessary, and it is important for a person to know how to choose the friend with whom he will spend his time and deliver his secrets. (Kuwait)

3) *The friendship / Friendship* is an essential relational aspect, surely one of the main foundations of *societies / society*, along with the family and *couples / the couple. Friends / The friends* can be such a great source of confidence, well-being and security that they determine our personality. (Spain)

4) Friendship can bring a sense of support to both parties, can help in times of difficulty, and make progress together, it brings strength to both sides. (China)

5) Friends are a fundamental part of our lives very little and until we are older. Trust in other people forms the fabric of society, for if we could not do this, society as we know it today would not be possible. (Hungary)

The five texts were translated by Google Translate. They have not been reviewd and contain some mistakes.

TEXT 1 Look at the pronouns in italics. Which ones are not correct? Why?

TEXT 2 This sentence is quite long. Can you divide it up into shorter sentences?

TEXT 3 Choose the correct form.

TEXT 4 AND 5 Rewrite the sentences so that the sense is clearer and so that they make grammatical sense.

The next three exercises are examples of tasks that you can set for homework.

10.10 Pronunciation

STEP 1 A simple way for students to check their pronunciation is for them to dictate into Microsoft Word a text containing the words that they have just studied.

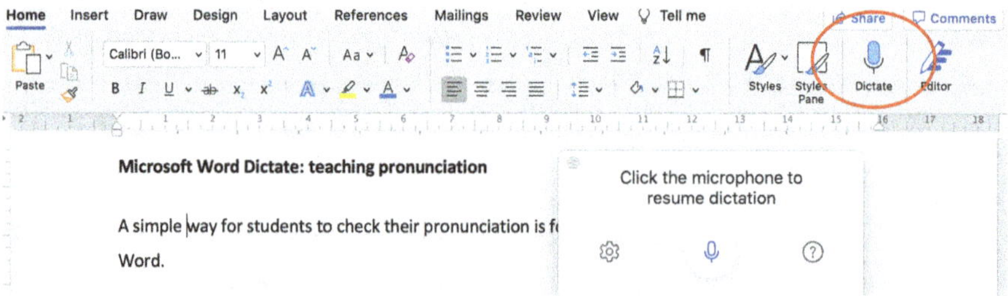

STEP 2 They can then see immediately if Word recognizes their pronunciation. If there are words that Word failed to recognize, then the student can check the pronunciation with an online dictionary such as Word Reference. Let's imagine that the word is *innovation*.

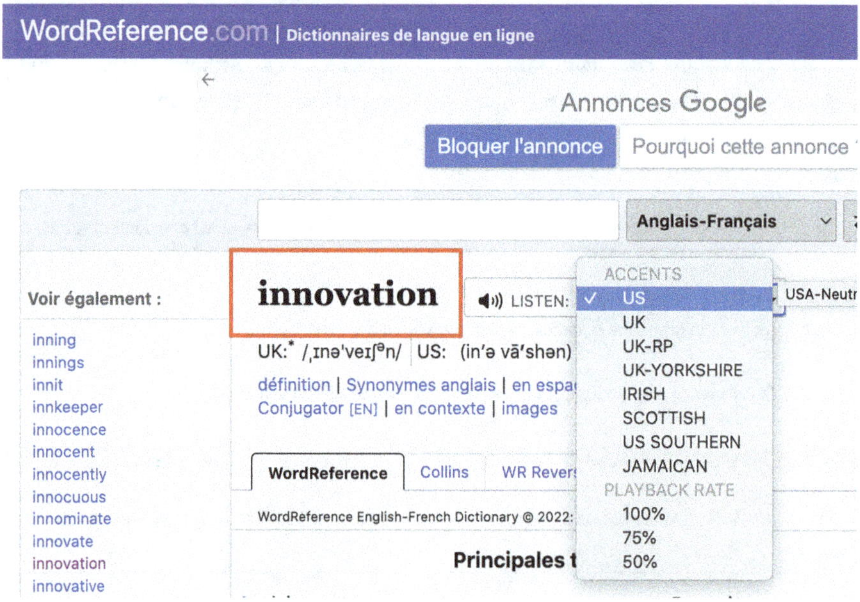

STEP 3 Student practises the mispronounced words until Dictate recognizes them.

Clearly STEP 2 involves showing students the features of WordReference, such as the fact that you don't simply get a definition, but also how the word is pronounced in GB and US English (and also in other varieties).

Possible issues: if I dictate the word *management* into Word using the wrong stress (i.e. on the second rather than the first syllable), Word may still recognize the mistaken pronunciation. But even if it does, this is a benefit because it proves to the student that although their pronunciation is not perfect, even if they do mispronounce certain words (typically those with multiple syllables) they can still be understood. This information is important to reassure a student who is about to do an oral presentation or take part in a Zoom.

Where Word may sometimes get it wrong is with vowel sounds: *war vs where, walk vs work*. In such case Word uses its usual system of underlining to indicate that something is wrong.

10.11 Merging two languages

You can type in two languages at the same time into the translation window and GT returns a homogeneous English version.

This is great for students who are sure about certain phrases in English, but not about others. The result is that students are highly motivated to see how GT translates the parts that they left in their own language. If the texts are sufficiently short, you can also do a quick check to confirm that GT got it right.

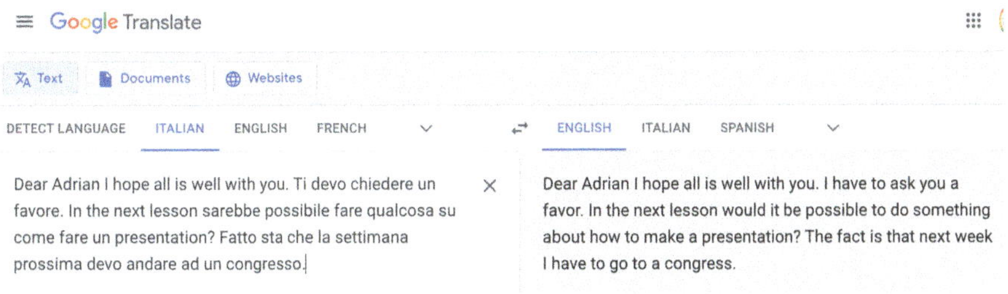
Google Translate
Text
Documents
Websites
DETECT LANGUAGE
ITALIAN
ENGLISH
FRENCH
ENGLISH
ITALIAN
SPANISH
Dear Adrian I hope all is well with you. Ti devo chiedere un favore. In the next lesson sarebbe possibile fare qualcosa su come fare un presentation? Fatto sta che la settimana prossima devo andare ad un congresso.
Dear Adrian I hope all is well with you. I have to ask you a favor. In the next lesson would it be possible to do something about how to make a presentation? The fact is that next week I have to go to a congress.

10.12 Checking whether a text was generated by a chatbot

If you are a member of the teaching staff or an editor of a journal and you want to check whether a text your student / a researcher has sent to you was generated at least in part by a bot, there are many bots that can supposedly help you. However, they tend to give really unhelpful answers such as:

Your text may include parts written by AI.

Your text is likely to be written entirely by a human.

Thus their answers contain a very low level of certainty (*may, likely*).

A fun exercise is to give students texts, some of which have been generated by a bot and some by a human. The students' task is to identify which ones were generated by AI and to list the clues. Emails work really well as examples.

As a teacher and editor the way I can see whether a student or researcher has used AI is if the text:

- is in perfect English
- is structured very logically
- follows a standard structure in terms of the order of the information given
- does not have concrete examples
- has more paragraphs than would be usual given the way people of the student's or researcher's nationality would normally use
- consistently uses sentences of around 20 words in length
- is rather boring (I quickly lose interest)

Back matter

More on using AI to help write research papers

To learn more about using ChatGPT and Google Translate in the specific context of writing a research paper for publication in an international journal, see Chapter 9 and Chapter 10 of *English for Writing Research Papers* (2023 edition). In the latter book you will also find explanations of how to use ChatGPT in each section of a paper:

Titles 10.17, Abstracts 12.13, 13.1, 13.9 Introduction 14.10, Review of the Literature 15.9, Methods 16.2, Results 17.9, Discussion 18.12–13, Conclusions 19.3, 19.10

For an updated list of prompts that you can use to generate texts, correct/edit texts, paraphrase/reduce texts get advice and recommendations on your text see my book dedicated to prompts and another book that I hope to write about Curie: https://www.springer.com/series/13913

A. Wallwork, *AI-Assisted Writing and Presenting in English*, English for Academic Research, https://doi.org/10.1007/978-3-031-48147-5

Other books in this series

There is a lot of cross-referencing in this book to the other books in the series and to materials that I have produced. This is both to save space in the current book, but also to enable you to find more details on particular aspects.

English for Writing Research Papers – everything you need to know about how to write a paper that referees will recommend for publication.

English for Research: Usage Style, and Grammar – covers those areas of English grammar that non-native academics tend to have difficulty with.

English for Academic Research: Writing Exercises

English for Academic Research: Vocabulary Exercises

English for Academic Research: Grammar Exercises

100 Tips to Avoid Mistakes in Academic Writing and Presenting – outlines the typical mistakes made in each section of a research paper; explains how to avoid redundancy and ambiguity; lists typical mistakes in proposals, journal submissions and emails; also tells you how to improve your presentation skills.

English for Presentations at International Conferences – all the tricks for overcoming your fears of presenting in English at a conference.

English for Academic Correspondence – tips for responding to editors and referees, networking at conferences, understanding fast-talking native English speakers, using Google Translate, and much more. No other book like this exists on the market.

English for Interacting on Campus – covers your daily activities as a university student: interacting with professors and other students, going to lectures, socializing, overcoming difficulties of living in a new country.

English for Academic CVs, Resumes, and Online Profiles – your CV / resume is probably the most important document that you write as an academic – it is the one that gets you jobs and funds.

English for Academic Research: A Guide for Teachers – written for EAP teachers. Tips on how to prepare English courses, plus insights into the academic world of research, congresses and publishing.

Online academic/scientific English course

I occasionally organize an online course via Zoom for PhD students and EAP teachers, which covers some or all of the following. How to:

- write a research paper
- do a presentation at an international conference
- use ChatGPT, Copilot, Gemini etc, Curie, and Google Translate, Deep L etc
- write emails, rebuttal letters, CVs/resumes

The courses are between 10–20 hours, take place at some time between 0800 and 1800 CET, and have a maximum number of 12 participants.

If you are interested please contact me (adrian.wallwork@gmail.com) and tell me who you are, where you are located, and times of day (CET) and periods of year when you are not available.

You can see feedback here.

Acknowledgements

Anna Southern for helping me revamp the first draft of this book; Jean Kollantai for her discussions on what editors and journals are looking for; Martin Cuss and Chrissie Mayer of the Plain English Campaign (whose first book is the inspiration behind the English for Academic Series), my father Basil Wallwork for instilling me with a fascination for the English language; and Maksim Ilyakhov and Ljudmila Sarycheva for confirming what I suspected – that all languages can be written in a simple way, the decision is the author's not the dictates of the language. I am grateful to the Italian Institute of Technology in Pontedera (Italy), some of whose materials I have revamped to produce the examples in Chapter 7.

About the author

Adrian Wallwork runs an agency specialized in editing and revising scientific papers. He also teaches English for Academic Purposes (EAP) to PhD students. In addition to his many books for Springer, he has written course books for Oxford University Press and discussion books for Cambridge University Press.

His passion is teaching PhD students and researchers how to write and present their research. He is also particularly interested in using the amazing advances in artificial intelligence to help students write and translate their work.

Full table of contents

Chapter 1 Being realistic about what AI can and cannot do

A. Wallwork, *AI-Assisted Writing and Presenting in English*, English for Academic Research, https://doi.org/10.1007/978-3-031-48147-5

Chapter 2 Prompts for correcting or paraphrasing your English

Chapter 3 Pre-editing

Chapter 4 Using a chatbot as a language editor to check your English

Chapter 5 How to interact with a chatbot, and simulate typical scenarios that take place in academia

Chapter 6 Communicating with lay audiences

Chapter 7 Presentations

Index[1]

[1] This index is by section number. Numbers in **bold** refer to complete chapters. This index does not include individual LLMs.

A. Wallwork, *AI-Assisted Writing and Presenting in English*, English for Academic Research, https://doi.org/10.1007/978-3-031-48147-5

www.ingramcontent.com/pod-product-compliance
Lightning Source LLC
LaVergne TN
LVHW012059290125
802503LV00025BA/262